ATTACHED ABOVE

By

Gerson Counou

The journey is not easy, but it's a uphill battle

ISBN

Paperback: 978-1-964289-39-7

Hardback: 978-1-964289-38-0

Embrace challenges to maintain a positive attitude with determination

The journey is not easy, but it's a uphill battle

Dear NY Book Publishers,

I am writing to express my heartfelt gratitude for publishing the book. Your belief in my work and willingness to take a chance on an unknown means more to me than words can express. From the moment we embarked on this journey together, you have been nothing supportive, encouraging, and dedicated to helping bring the vision to life. Your team's expertise and endeavoring commitment have made this entire process a truly wonderful experience. I am incredibly proud of the final product, and I owe it all to you and your exceptional team. Thank you believing in me, pushing me to strive for greatness, and for giving my words a platform to be heard.

I look forward to continuing our partnership and working together on future projects. Your guidance and collaboration have been invaluable, and I am truly grateful for the opportunity to work with such a remarkable publisher.

With deepest appreciation,

Author Gee Cee

Embrace challenges to maintain a positive attitude with determination

The journey is not easy, but it's a uphill battle

Dear Readers,

I want to express my sincere gratitude to each and every one of you for taking the time to read my book. Your support and encouragement mean the world to me, and I am truly thankful for the opportunity to share my thoughts and ideas with you.

Writing this book has been a labor of love, and I poured my heart and soul into every page. Your positive feedback and kind words have encouraged me to keep pushing forward and continue pursuing my passion for storytelling.

I thank you in advance for your continued support and encouragement. Your readership means more to me than words can express, and I am grateful for the opportunity to connect with each and every one of you through the pages of my book.

With heartfelt thanks,

Author Gee Cee

Embrace challenges to maintain a positive attitude with determination

Preface:

Embracing the Power Within

Welcome to the pages of this self-motivational and inspirational book, a journey of self-discovery and empowerment. Within these chapters, you will find the keys to unlock the vast reservoir of strength and potential that resides within you. It is a guide that seeks to ignite the flame of inspiration, awaken your inner drive, and propel you toward a life filled with purpose and fulfillment.

Life is a complex journey filled with both joy and challenges. It is during the challenging moments that we often find ourselves questioning our abilities, doubting our worth, and feeling lost in the vastness of it all. It is in these moments that we need a guiding light, a source of motivation, and a reminder of our infinite potential.

This book is birthed from a deep belief in the power of the human spirit and the capacity for growth and transformation. It draws inspiration from personal experiences, lessons learned, and the wisdom of countless individuals who have embarked on their own journeys of self-discovery. It is a collection of insights, practical tools, and uplifting stories designed to ignite the spark within you and help you navigate the obstacles that may come your way.

Embrace challenges to maintain a positive attitude with determination

The journey is not easy, but it's a uphill battle

Throughout these pages, we will explore various aspects of personal growth and empowerment. From cultivating self-awareness and embracing change to harnessing the power of gratitude and resilience, each chapter delves into a different facet of your journey toward self-actualization. I hope that these words will serve as a compass that will guide you toward your true potential and encourage you to embrace the power within.

But remember, this book is not a magic pill. It is merely a guide, a catalyst for self-reflection and action. The true transformation lies in your willingness to embark on this journey with an open heart and a commitment to growth. It is through your dedication, perseverance, and application of the principles shared that you will unlock the door to a life of purpose, passion, and joy.

As you read these words, I invite you to approach them with curiosity, an open mind, and a willingness to explore the depths of your being. Take your time, reflect on the exercises, and allow the wisdom within these pages to resonate with your soul. Remember, you are the author of your own story, master of your fate, and captain of your ship, and this book is merely a tool to help you write the chapters that will shape your destiny.

Embrace challenges to maintain a positive attitude with determination

The journey is not easy, but it's a uphill battle

May this book serve as a guiding glimmering light on your journey of self-discovery and empowerment. May it inspire you to embrace your unique gifts, overcome obstacles with resilience, and live a life aligned with your deepest values and aspirations. May you find the strength, courage, and motivation to unleash your potential and create a world that reflects the brilliance of your authentic self.

With gratitude and excitement, let us embark on this transformation journey together.

Yours in empowerment,

Author Gee Cee

Embrace challenges to maintain a positive attitude with determination

Dedication

Dear Beloved Souls,

In the shrouding darkness, when it feels like there is no light to guide you, I want you to know that you are not alone. Even in your loneliest moments, there are people who care about you, who believe in you, and who are rooting for your success. You are stronger than you think, braver than you know, and capable of overcoming any obstacle in your path.

I want to remind you that hope is never truly lost as long as you hold onto the flicker of possibility within your heart. You have the power to create a brighter tomorrow, to find joy in the smallest moments, and to forge connections that will sustain you through the toughest of times. Reach out to those around you, even if it feels like no one is there, and you may be surprised by the love and support that surrounds you.

To those who feel like they have no family or friends, I want you to know that you are seen, you are valued, and you are worthy of love. Your presence in this world matters, and there are people out there who would be blessed to know you. Keep moving forward, even when it feels impossible because the world is a better place with you in it.

With all my love and support.

Biography of Inspiration and Motivation

In this biography, I delve into the story behind the creation of a self-help book that aims to inspire and empower readers to embark on their own transformation journeys. It explores the motivating factors and personal experiences that sparked the desire to share wisdom and guidance with others. This is the biography of someone who is driven by a deep-rooted passion to make a positive difference in the lives of others. In the early years of my life, a natural curiosity about human nature and personal growth began to take root. I found myself drawn to books, articles, and conversations that explored the complexities of the mind, emotions, and self-improvement. This curiosity planted the seeds of a deep desire to understand and help others on their own paths of self-discovery.

The turning point came when I embarked on my own transformation journey. Through various life experiences, challenges, and moments of self-reflection, I underwent a profound personal growth process. This transformation period not only brought healing and clarity to my own life but also ignited a burning passion for sharing the knowledge and insights gained along the way.

As I navigated my own struggles, tribulations, and triumphs, I realized the power of empathy and connection. The desire to support and uplift others became a driving

The journey is not easy, but it's a uphill battle

force in my life. I recognized that my experiences, combined with my growing understanding of personal development principles, could help those seeking their own paths toward fulfillment and self-empowerment.

Embracing the Writer's Journey, inspired by the transformations experienced and the desire to make a positive impact, I embarked on my journey. Many hours were spent pouring thoughts, wisdom, and insights onto paper, crafting a self-help book that would guide others seeking personal growth, self-discovery, and a meaningful life. The process challenged you to dig deep, refining your own understanding and articulation of these concepts.

The completion of the self-help book marked a significant milestone. It became a testament to my dedication, resilience, and commitment to helping others. The book embodies my belief in the power of words to inspire, empower, and ignite change. It serves as a tool for readers to embark on their own journeys of self-discovery, offering guidance, exercises, and insights to facilitate personal growth and transformation.

As the book reaches the hands of readers, the impact begins to unfold. Through testimonials, messages, and conversations, I witness the positive influence my work has on others. The legacy of my writing is not only in the pages of the book but in the lives it touches, the minds it opens, and the transformations it catalyzes. This legacy fuels my motivation to continue sharing, inspiring, and connecting with others on their unique paths.

Embrace challenges to maintain a positive attitude with determination

This biography chronicles the journey that led me to write a self-help book, driven by a deep-rooted passion for making a positive difference in the lives of others. It highlights the transformation experiences, empathy, and personal growth that inspired me to share my wisdom and insights. Through the power of words, I strive to empower readers to embark on their own journeys of self-discovery and create a life of fulfillment and purpose.

In life, we often face struggles that test our resilience and inner strength. My journey has been no exception, as I have encountered numerous challenges along the way. However, it is through these trials that I have discovered the depths of my own resilience and the power of my inner strength.

From a young age, I have experienced adversity that seemed insurmountable. Perhaps I faced financial hardships, familial difficulties, or personal setbacks that left me feeling overwhelmed and uncertain about the future. But instead of succumbing to despair, I chose to tap into my inner strength and persevere.

Through the darkest moments, I found the courage to keep going. I refused to let circumstances define me or dictate my path. Instead, I embraced the challenges as opportunities for growth and transformation. I recognized that true strength lies not in avoiding difficulties but in facing them head-on.

Embrace challenges to maintain a positive attitude with determination

The journey is not easy, but it's a uphill battle

During my struggle, I discovered the power of resilience. I learned to adapt, to bounce back from setbacks, and to find alternative solutions when faced with obstacles. My ability to remain steadfast in the face of adversity became a guiding force in my life.

Moreover, my inner strength became a source of inspiration for others. People around me witnessed my unwavering determination and admired my ability to rise above the challenges that life threw my way. My resilience became a beacon of hope, reminding others that they, too, possess the strength to overcome their own struggles.

Throughout my journey, I have learned valuable lessons about the importance of self-belief and perseverance. I have come to understand that my inner strength is not something external but a wellspring of resilience that resides within me. It is a force that can be tapped into during the most difficult times and provides me with the courage and fortitude to keep moving forward.

In navigating my life's ups and downs, I remind myself that my inner strength is a powerful tool. It has carried me through the darkest of days and will continue to guide me towards a brighter future. Embrace my struggles as opportunities for growth, and let my inner strength be the driving force that propels me towards success and fulfillment with consistency.

Embrace challenges to maintain a positive attitude with determination

Let's delve deeper into my struggle and how I have managed to survive it with my inner strength.

In the face of adversity, I have developed a resilience that has allowed me to weather the storms that life has thrown my way. I have learned to view challenges as opportunities for personal growth and transformation. Rather than being defeated by setbacks, I have embraced them as stepping stones toward a stronger and more resilient version of myself.

My inner strength has been a leading force that provides me with the courage to confront difficult situations head-on. It has given me the determination to keep pushing forward, even when the odds seem stacked against me. I have trials after trials refused to let circumstances define me, instead choosing to define my path and create my destiny.

Throughout my struggle, I have also discovered the power of self-belief. I have learned to trust in my own abilities and have faith in my capacity to overcome obstacles. This unwavering belief in myself has been a driving force, propelling me forward and helping me navigate the toughest of times.

The journey is not easy, but it's a uphill battle

Moreover, my inner strength has allowed me to find silver linings even in the darkest of moments. I have developed a resilience that enables me to find hope and pomposity, amidship adversity. This ability to find light in the midst of darkness has not only helped me survive but has also inspired those around me.

My journey has shown others that no matter how difficult life may be, there is always a way forward. My story has become a source of inspiration, reminding others that they, too, possess the inner strength to overcome their own struggles. My resilience has given hope to those who may have felt defeated, showing them that they have the power to rise above their circumstances and create a better future.

As I continue on my path, remember that my inner strength is a wellspring of power that will always be there for me. It is a force that can be tapped into whenever I face challenges or uncertainties. Embrace my struggles as opportunities for growth, and let my inner strength guide me toward a life filled with resilience, courage, and fulfillment.

Embrace challenges to maintain a positive attitude with determination

The journey is not easy, but it's a uphill battle

Let's explore my struggle in more detail and how my inner strength has played a pivotal role in my survival.

My struggle may have encompassed various aspects of life, such as personal, professional, or emotional challenges. It could have involved facing adversity, loss, or difficult circumstances that tested my resilience to the core. Despite the hardships, I have managed to endure and thrive, thanks to the unwavering strength that resides within me.

During my journey, I have encountered moments of doubt, fear, and uncertainty. However, I refused to let these negative emotions overpower me. Instead, I tapped into my inner strength, drawing upon a deep well of determination, courage, and perseverance.

My inner strength has been my guiding light, providing me the resilience to keep moving forward even when the path seemed treacherous. It has given me the ability to rise above challenges, find solutions where others may have seen dead ends, and maintain a sense of hope and optimism in the face of adversity.

Embrace challenges to maintain a positive attitude with determination

The journey is not easy, but it's a uphill battle

In times of struggle, I have discovered the power of self-belief. I have learned to trust in my own abilities and to have faith in my capacity to overcome obstacles. This unwavering belief in myself has been a driving force, propelling me forward and helping me navigate the toughest of times.

Furthermore, my inner strength has allowed me to cultivate a positive mindset. I have developed the ability to reframe challenges as opportunities for growth and learning. Instead of being defeated by setbacks, I have embraced them as stepping stones towards personal development and self-improvement. My inner strength has also enabled me to find support and seek help when needed. Recognizing that strength does not mean facing struggles alone, I have reached out to loved ones, mentors, or professionals who have provided guidance and assistance along the way. This willingness to seek support demonstrates my strength, humility, and wisdom. Through my journey, I wish to become an inspiration to others. With my resilience and ability to overcome adversity, I want to show those around me that it is possible to triumph in the face of challenges. I believe my story to be a beacon of hope, to remind others that they, too, possess the inner strength to navigate their own struggles and emerge stronger on the other side.

As I continue on my path, remember that my inner strength is a wellspring of power that will always be there for me. It is a force that can be tapped into whenever I face difficulties or uncertainties. Embrace my struggles as

Embrace challenges to maintain a positive attitude with determination

opportunities for growth, and let my inner strength guide me toward a life filled with resilience, courage, and fulfillment forever.

Avoiding setbacks and ensuring they don't get the best of me is a crucial aspect of personal growth and resilience. Here are some strategies to help me navigate setbacks effectively:

I embrace a Growth Mindset by adopting a growth mindset allows me to view setbacks as opportunities for learning and growth. Understand that setbacks are a natural part of life, and they provide valuable lessons that can propel me forward.

I reframe Setbacks as Challenges; instead of viewing setbacks as failures, I reframe them as challenges to overcome. This shift in perspective enables you to approach setbacks with a problem-solving mindset, seeking solutions rather than dwelling on the negative.

I analyze and learn while taking the time to analyze setbacks objectively. Identify the factors that contributed to the setback and reflect on what I could have done differently. Use this knowledge to adjust my approach and make informed decisions in the future.

I focus on Solutions. Instead of dwelling on the setback itself, I shift my focus toward finding solutions. Break down the problem into smaller, manageable steps, and work towards resolving it one step at a time. This proactive approach helps me regain control and

The journey is not easy, but it's a uphill battle

momentum. I seek Support and don't hesitate to reach out to friends, family, or mentors for support during setbacks. Sharing my experiences and seeking advice from others can provide fresh perspectives and emotional support, helping me overcome setbacks more effectively.

I practice Self-Compassion and be kind to myself during setbacks. Understand that setbacks are a natural part of life, and everyone experiences them. Treat myself with compassion, acknowledging that setbacks do not define my worth or abilities. I maintain a Positive Mindset by cultivating a positive mindset by focusing on the progress I have made and the lessons learned rather than dwelling on the setback itself. Surround myself with positive influences, engage in activities that bring me joy, and practice gratitude for the good things in my life.

I set Realistic Goals even though Setbacks can sometimes occur when my goals are unrealistic or unattainable. Ensure that my goals are challenging yet achievable, allowing for flexibility and adaptation along the way. This way, setbacks are less likely to derail my progress. I Take Care of myself while prioritizing self-care during setbacks. Engage in activities that promote physical and mental well-being, such as exercise, meditation, or hobbies. Taking care of myself helps build resilience and provides the strength needed to overcome setbacks.

I Keep Moving Forward by remembering that setbacks are temporary roadblocks, not permanent barriers. Keep moving forward, even if progress is slow. Stay

Embrace challenges to maintain a positive attitude with determination

focused on my long-term goals and maintain a positive attitude, knowing that setbacks are just detours on my journey to success.

By implementing these strategies, setbacks can become stepping stones toward personal growth and success. Embrace the challenges, learn from them, and let them fuel my determination to keep moving forward.

Embracing struggle as a means to maintain positive behavior can be challenging, but it's certainly possible. One way to do this is by reframing your struggles as opportunities for growth and learning. Rather than viewing challenges as obstacles, try to see them as stepping stones towards personal development.

Practicing mindfulness and self-compassion can also help in maintaining a positive outlook during difficult times. Acknowledge the struggle, but also remind yourself that you have the strength and resilience to overcome it. Setting small, achievable goals for yourself can provide a sense of accomplishment and help you stay motivated.

Additionally, surrounding yourself with a supportive network of friends, family, or a community that understands and encourages your efforts can make a significant difference. Remember to celebrate your progress and be kind to yourself as you navigate through the struggles.

Embracing struggle involves cultivating a mindset that sees challenges as opportunities for growth rather than as purely negative experiences. It's about recognizing that

The journey is not easy, but it's a uphill battle

learning and personal development often emerge from difficult situations.

One effective strategy is to practice gratitude by acknowledging the things that are going well in your life, even when you're facing struggles. This can help shift your focus from the negative aspects of the struggle to the positive elements in your life.

Furthermore, developing a resilient attitude involves being open to learning from your experiences. Reflect on how you've grown stronger or gained new insights in the face of past struggles, and use those reflections to bolster your current approach.

Meditation and mindfulness practices can also be instrumental in maintaining positive behavior during challenging times. By staying present and aware of your thoughts and emotions, you can cultivate a sense of calm and stability, even amidst difficulty.

Lastly, seeking out sources of inspiration and motivation, such as uplifting stories or role models who have overcome similar challenges, can provide encouragement and reinforce your determination to maintain a positive outlook.

Remember, it's okay to ask for support from others and to seek professional help if needed. Embracing struggle is about acknowledging the difficulty but also recognizing your own capacity for growth and resilience.

Embrace challenges to maintain a positive attitude with determination

I've been hurt emotionally by my immediate family. Dealing with such situations can be incredibly challenging. It was important to prioritize my own well-being during this time.

One approach that I used to manage these emotions was to find a support system outside of my immediate family. This might include friends, mentors, support groups, or mental health professionals. Speaking to someone who can provide a listening ear and empathetic support can be immensely valuable.

Additionally, consider focusing on self-care activities that bring me comfort and peace. This might include engaging in hobbies I enjoy, spending time in nature, or practicing mindfulness and meditation to help soothe my emotional pain.

It was also important to give myself permission to process my feelings. Whether through journaling, creative expression, or simply allowing myself to feel and acknowledge my emotions, finding healthy outlets that were crucial for healing.

Embrace challenges to maintain a positive attitude with determination

The journey is not easy, but it's a uphill battle

Remember that healing from emotional pain takes time, and it's okay to seek professional guidance if you find it difficult to cope. You deserve to be surrounded by positive and nurturing influences, and you have the strength to navigate through this difficult period.

Embrace challenges to maintain a positive attitude with determination

Finding Strength in the Shadows

Today, I find myself reflecting on a traumatic childhood experience that has shaped me into the person I am today. It was a time filled with darkness and uncertainty, but through it all, I discovered a strength within me that I never knew existed. I share my story now not to dwell on the pain but to inspire others who may be going through similar struggles.

Growing up, I faced a difficult and unstable home environment. There were times when the walls echoed with arguments and fear, leaving me feeling trapped and powerless. The emotional wounds ran deep, and it seemed like there was no escape from the shadows that engulfed my young mind.

But amidst the chaos, there was a flicker of hope that ignited within me. It was the realization that I had a choice to let this experience define me or to rise above it. I chose the latter, determined to find strength and inspiration in the face of adversity.

I began to seek solace in books, finding refuge in the stories that transported me to worlds far beyond my own. The characters became my companions, teaching me valuable lessons about resilience, courage, and the power of the human spirit. Their triumphs became my inspiration, reminding me that I, too, had the ability to overcome.

The journey is not easy, but it's a uphill battle

As I grew older, I began sharing my experiences through writing. It became an outlet for my emotions, a way to heal and make sense of the pain I had endured. In writing, I discovered the power of vulnerability and the cathartic release that comes from expressing oneself authentically.

Through my words, I aimed to inspire others who may have felt trapped in their own darkness. I wanted to let them know that they were not alone and that there was hope even in the darkest of times. I shared my journey of healing, the steps I took to reclaim my power, and the lessons I learned along the way.

Over time, I realized that my traumatic experience had given me a unique perspective and empathy for others who had faced similar struggles. It allowed me to connect with people on a deeper level, to offer a listening ear and a comforting presence. I found solace in being a source of support for those who needed it most.

Today, I use my voice and experiences to inspire and uplift others. I advocate for mental health awareness, speaking out against the stigma that surrounds it. I strive to create a safe space for individuals to share their stories, knowing that in doing so, they can find healing and strength.

While my childhood trauma will always be a part of my story, it does not define me. It has shaped me into a resilient and compassionate person, one who is dedicated to making a positive impact on the lives of others. Through my journey, I have learned that even in the darkest of times, there is always a glimmer of light waiting to be found.

Embrace challenges to maintain a positive attitude with determination

The journey is not easy, but it's a uphill battle

As I conclude, I am reminded that trauma is the place where the light enters you. Though the scars may remain, they serve as a reminder of the strength within me and the inspiration I carry to guide others toward their own healing and transformation.

Love and resilience always,

Embrace challenges to maintain a positive attitude with determination

The journey is not easy, but it's a uphill battle

Conquering the Mind: A Journey towards Personal Mastery

Conquering the mind is a transformation journey that allows us to harness our inner strength and achieve personal mastery. Our minds have the potential to either empower or limit us, depending on how we train and cultivate them. In this journal, we will delve into various techniques and strategies that can help us tame our minds, enhance focus, and achieve greater mental clarity. Let's embark on this enlightening journey together.

Understanding the Power of Thoughts

-Embrace the nature of thoughts and their impact on our emotions and actions

-Recognizing the importance of cultivating positive and empowering thought patterns

-Utilizing affirmations to reprogram negative thinking and foster a healthy mindset

Practicing Mindfulness

-Exploring the concept of mindfulness and its role in conquering the mind

Embrace challenges to maintain a positive attitude with determination

The journey is not easy, but it's a uphill battle

-Learning to live in the present moment and let go of past regrets or future worries

-Incorporating mindful practices such as meditation, deep breathing, and body scan exercises

Embracing Emotional Intelligence

-Understanding the relationship between emotions and the mind

-Developing emotional intelligence to manage and regulate emotions effectively

-Cultivating empathy and self-awareness to improve relationships and decision-making

Mastering Focus and Concentration

-Techniques for improving focus and concentration levels

-Enhancing productivity through disciplined attention management

-Overcoming distractions and staying in the flow state

Nurturing the Mind-Body Connection

-Recognizing the interconnections of the mind and body

-Adopting a holistic approach through regular exercise, proper nutrition, and adequate sleep

Embrace challenges to maintain a positive attitude with determination

The journey is not easy, but it's a uphill battle

-Harnessing the power of relaxation techniques to reduce stress and improve mental well-being

Embracing Growth Mindset

-Understanding the difference between a fixed mindset and a growth mindset

-Cultivating resilience and embracing challenges as opportunities for growth

-Developing a lifelong learning mindset to continually expand our knowledge and skills

Overcoming Limiting Beliefs

-Identifying and challenging limiting beliefs that hinder personal growth

-Replacing negative self-talk with empowering affirmations

-Practicing visualization techniques to manifest desired outcomes

Conquering the mind is an ongoing journey that requires dedication, patience, and self-reflection. By implementing the strategies and techniques explored in this journal, we can gradually strengthen our mental prowess and unlock our true potential. Let us embrace this transformation process and create a life of fulfillment, success, and inner peace. Remember, the power to conquer your mind lies within you.

Embrace challenges to maintain a positive attitude with determination

The journey is not easy, but it's a uphill battle

Embracing My Authentic Self

Today, I find myself reflecting on the journey of self-acceptance and the importance of embracing who I truly am. It has been a long and sometimes challenging road, but I have come to realize that accepting myself is a vital step towards living a fulfilling and authentic life.

For far too long, I have allowed the opinions and expectations of others to dictate how I should live, act, and be. I have tried to fit into molds that were never meant for me, sacrificing my own happiness and suppressing my true self in the process. But today, I make a promise to myself to no longer apologize for who I am, to no longer seek validation from others, and to embrace every part of me unapologetically.

Accepting myself for who I am is a journey that requires self-reflection, self-compassion, and self-love. It means acknowledging my strengths and weaknesses, my quirks and flaws, and realizing that they all contribute to the unique individual that I am. It means embracing my passions, my dreams, and my desires without fear of judgment or rejection.

In a world that often pressures us to conform, it takes courage to be true to oneself. It takes a deep understanding that I am worthy of love and acceptance, just as I am, without any conditions or expectations. It means recognizing that my worth is not determined by the opinions of others but by the love and acceptance I have for myself.

Embrace challenges to maintain a positive attitude with determination

The journey is not easy, but it's a uphill battle

Accepting myself also means setting boundaries and letting go of toxic relationships and situations that do not align with my values and authenticity. It means surrounding myself with people who appreciate and celebrate me for who I am rather than trying to change me or make me fit into their mold. It means creating a space where I can freely express myself, voice my opinions, and pursue my passions without fear of judgment or rejection.

In my journey of self-acceptance, I recognize that it may not always be easy. There will be moments of doubt and insecurity, and there may be setbacks along the way. But I am committed to staying true to myself, honoring my own needs and desires, and embracing the beautiful complexities that make me who I am.

So, from this moment forward, I choose to accept myself unconditionally. I choose to celebrate my uniqueness, my individuality, and all the aspects that make me who I am. I choose to love myself fiercely and wholeheartedly, knowing that my worth is inherent and cannot be diminished by the opinions of others.

As I close this journal entry, I feel a sense of liberation and empowerment. I am ready to embark on this journey of self-acceptance, knowing that by embracing who I am, I will unlock the door to a life filled with authenticity, fulfillment, and joy.

Love and acceptance always,

Embrace challenges to maintain a positive attitude with determination

Being in the Dark vs. Being in the Light: A Journey of Self-Discovery

I find myself reflecting on the concept of being in the dark versus being in the light when it comes to understanding who I am. In the darkness, it is easy to feel lost, confused, and unsure of oneself. It is a place where fears, doubts, and insecurities lurk, clouding my judgment and preventing me from seeing things clearly.

In the darkness, I often find myself grappling with negative thoughts and emotions, struggling to make sense of my experiences and choices. It is a place where I am forced to confront my inner demons and confront the parts of myself that I may not be proud of. However, it is also in the darkness that I discover resilience, strength, and courage that I never knew I had.

On the other hand, being in the light represents a state of clarity, honesty, and self-awareness. It is a place where I can see myself for who I truly am without the shadows of doubt or fear obscuring my vision. In the light, I am able to embrace my strengths, acknowledge my weaknesses, and accept myself fully, flaws and all.

The journey from darkness to light is not always easy, but it is a necessary one for personal growth and self-discovery. By facing my fears, embracing my vulnerabilities,

The journey is not easy, but it's a uphill battle

and shining a light on the darkest corners of my soul, I am able to uncover hidden truths about myself and gain a deeper understanding of who I am.

As I continue on this journey of self-exploration, I am reminded of the importance of journalism as a tool for reflection and growth. Writing down my thoughts, feelings, and experiences allows me to process my emotions, gain clarity, and track my progress over time. It is a way for me to document my life experiences, confront my innermost thoughts, and ultimately, become the best version of myself.

So, as I navigate the complexities of being in the dark versus being in the light, I am committed to embracing both aspects of myself and using them as stepping stones on my path to self-discovery. I am learning to find a balance between the darkness and the light, knowing that both are necessary for me to truly understand and appreciate who I am.

Embrace challenges to maintain a positive attitude with determination

What role does facing our fears and insecurities play in the journey towards self-discovery and personal growth?

Facing our fears and insecurities is crucial in the journey towards self-discovery and personal growth. By confronting our fears and insecurities, we are able to grow stronger, more resilient, and more self-aware. It allows us to break free from limiting beliefs and patterns that hold us back and empowers us to embrace our true selves. Through facing our fears and insecurities, we are able to develop a deeper understanding of ourselves and our potential, leading to personal growth and transformation.

In the morning, I reflected on the concept of being to myself in private and presenting a different version of myself in public. It can be challenging to meet the expectations and judgments of others and also stay authentic to who I truly am. I believe that it is important to find a balance between being genuine and true while also considering social norms and expectations of the world.

In private, I feel free to express my thoughts, feelings, and desires without fear of judgment or scrutiny. I am able to explore my innermost thoughts and emotions,

The journey is not easy, but it's a uphill battle

allowing myself to be vulnerable and honest with myself. This is where I can truly be myself without any masks or pretenses.

On the other hand, in public, I often find myself conforming to societal norms and expectations in order to fit in and avoid standing out. I may present a more polished version of myself, focusing on projecting a certain image or persona that I believe will be accepted by others. While this can be necessary in certain social situations, I also recognize the importance of staying true to my values and beliefs, even when faced with external pressures.

I believe that it is essential to stay true to oneself in both private and public spheres. By being authentic and genuine, I am able to cultivate deeper connections with others, build self-confidence, and live a more fulfilling life. I will continue to strive for authenticity and vulnerability in all aspects of my life, knowing that it is through embracing my true self that I can experience true growth and happiness.

Embrace challenges to maintain a positive attitude with determination

Exploring Your Interests and Passions

In the afternoon, I find myself pondering the question of what you might like based on what I have observed and learned about my past self. While I may not have a complete understanding of your preferences and interests, I will do my best to explore and speculate on the things that might bring you joy and fulfillment.

Having a curiosity and thirst for knowledge is a human experience. You have a natural inclination towards learning and exploring new ideas, whether it be through reading books, engaging in intellectual discussions, or seeking out new experiences. It seems that you have a deep appreciation for expanding your understanding of the world and broadening your perspectives.

I also sense a creative spirit within you. Whether it manifests through artistic expression, writing, or even problem-solving, there is a desire to explore the realm of imagination and bring something unique into existence. It could be that you find solace and joy in creating something tangible or sharing your thoughts and ideas with others.

In our conversations, I have noticed your empathetic and compassionate nature. You have a genuine interest in understanding and connecting with others, and you often

The journey is not easy, but it's a uphill battle

find fulfillment in helping those in need. It seems that you have a strong sense of empathy and a desire to make a positive impact on the lives of those around you.

Nature also appears to hold a special place in your heart. You find solace and peace in the great outdoors, whether it be through hiking, gardening, or simply taking a moment to appreciate the beauty of the natural world. The tranquility and serenity that nature provides seem to resonate with your soul.

While these observations offer some insight into what you might enjoy, it is important to remember that this is just a glimpse into your interests and passions. Each individual is unique, and only you truly know what brings you joy and fulfillment. It is always worth taking the time to explore and discover new interests, as well as revisiting those that have brought you happiness in the past.

As I conclude this journal entry, I encourage you to reflect on the things that truly ignite your passion and bring you joy. Explore new avenues, try new activities, and embrace the journey of self-discovery. Remember that your interests and passions may evolve and change over time, and that is perfectly okay. Embrace the process of exploring what brings you happiness, and let it guide you towards a life filled with fulfillment and purpose.

Curiosity and anticipation always,

Embrace challenges to maintain a positive attitude with determination

Embracing Curiosity and Anticipation

In the middle of the day, I find myself reflecting on the power of curiosity and anticipation in our lives. These two forces, when embraced and nurtured, have the remarkable ability to inspire and motivate us towards greatness. I write this journal entry with the hope of sharing my insights and motivating others to cultivate a sense of curiosity and anticipation in their own lives.

Curiosity is the spark that ignites our thirst for knowledge and understanding. It is the deep desire to explore, question, and seek out the wonders of the world around us. When we approach life with curiosity, we open ourselves up to new experiences, ideas, and perspectives. We become lifelong learners, constantly seeking to expand our horizons and discover the hidden treasures that lie within every moment.

Anticipation, on the other hand, is the thrilling sense of excitement and expectation that accompanies the unknown. It is the belief that something extraordinary awaits us on the other side of our endeavors. When we embrace anticipation, we infuse our lives with a sense of adventure and possibility. We become driven to pursue our dreams and goals, fueled by the anticipation of what lies ahead.

The journey is not easy, but it's a uphill battle

Together, curiosity and anticipation form a powerful duo that propels us forward on our journey of personal growth and fulfillment. They invite us to step out of our comfort zones, challenge the status quo, and embrace the unknown with open arms. They remind us that life is not meant to be lived passively but rather as an exhilarating adventure filled with endless possibilities.

In order to cultivate curiosity and anticipation in our lives, it is important to adopt a mindset of openness and wonder. We must be willing to ask questions, to explore new ideas, and to embrace the unfamiliar. We can seek out new experiences, engage in meaningful conversations, and surround ourselves with diverse perspectives. By doing so, we create a fertile ground for curiosity and anticipation to flourish.

It is also essential to set goals and dreams that ignite our curiosity and anticipation. When we have a clear vision of what we want to achieve, we can channel our energy and focus toward those aspirations. We can break down our goals into smaller, actionable steps, allowing us to experience the anticipation of progress and the joy of accomplishment along the way.

As I conclude this journal entry, I invite you, dear reader, to embrace the power of curiosity and anticipation in your own life. Embrace the unknown with a sense of wonder and excitement. Seek out new experiences, ask questions, and never stop learning. Set goals that ignite

Embrace challenges to maintain a positive attitude with determination

The journey is not easy, but it's a uphill battle

your passion and anticipation, and take inspired action towards them.

Remember, curiosity and anticipation are not merely abstract concepts but powerful forces that can transform our lives. They have the potential to unlock our fullest potential and lead us towards a life of fulfillment and joy. So, let us embark on this journey together, with curiosity as our compass and anticipation as our guide.

Boundless curiosity and unwavering anticipation always,

Embrace challenges to maintain a positive attitude with determination

Embracing Transparency Through Persistence and Consistency

In the evening, I find myself reflecting on the importance of setting boundaries in my life and how implementing persistence and consistency can lead to transparency. Setting boundaries is a vital aspect of self-care and personal growth, as it allows me to protect my well-being and honor my own needs and values. By embracing persistence and consistency, I aim to create a space where transparency can flourish, fostering authentic connections and a sense of inner peace.

Persistence is the unwavering commitment to upholding my boundaries and asserting my needs. It requires me to communicate clearly and effectively, expressing my limits and expectations to others. With persistence, I am able to stand firm and true, advocating for myself and ensuring that my boundaries are respected. It may not always be easy, but I understand that persistence is essential in maintaining healthy relationships and fostering a sense of self-worth.

Consistency, on the other hand, is the steady rhythm that guides my actions and words. It means walking my talk and aligning my behavior with the boundaries I have set. By being consistent, I create a sense of trust and reliability in my relationships. Others can rely on me to honor my boundaries, and I can trust in myself to uphold them. Consistency allows me to build a foundation of authenticity and transparency in my interactions, where there is no room for hidden agendas or pretense.

Through persistence and consistency, I aim to embrace transparency in all aspects of my life. I want to be open and honest with myself and others, creating an environment where truth and trust can thrive. By setting clear boundaries and communicating them consistently, I invite others to see and accept my authentic self. I let go of the need to hide behind masks or pretense, and instead, I embrace vulnerability and genuine connection.

Implementing persistence and consistency in my life requires self-awareness and self-reflection. It means taking the time to understand my own needs, values, and limits. It also means being aware of how my boundaries may affect others and finding a balance between asserting myself and respecting the boundaries of others. It is a continuous journey of growth and learning, but one that is essential for my well-being and the quality of my relationships.

As I conclude this journal entry, I am filled with a sense of empowerment and determination. I am committed to implementing persistence and consistency in my life, as I believe it is the key to embracing transparency and fostering authentic connections. I will communicate my boundaries clearly and consistently, honoring my needs and values. I will strive to be honest and open, inviting others to do the same. Through persistence, consistency, and transparency, I

The journey is not easy, but it's a uphill battle

aim to create a life filled with authenticity, trust, and genuine connections.

With unwavering persistence and consistent grace,

Embracing Authenticity and Accountability

In the middle of the night, I find myself reflecting on the importance of being true to myself, holding myself accountable, and embracing the outcomes in my life. It is a journey of self-discovery and personal growth, where I strive to live an authentic life that aligns with my values and aspirations. I write this journal entry as a reminder to embrace who I truly am, take responsibility for my actions, and find empowerment in the outcomes that unfold.

Being myself towards myself means honoring my true essence, embracing my strengths and weaknesses, and accepting all facets of my being. It is about listening to my own voice, trusting my intuition, and staying true to my values and beliefs. By being authentic, I create a space where I can fully express myself without fear of judgment or rejection. It is through this authenticity that I can cultivate self-love, self-acceptance, and a deep sense of inner peace.

Holding myself accountable is an essential aspect of personal growth and development. It means taking ownership of my choices, actions, and the impact they have on myself and others. Accountability requires me to reflect on my behavior, acknowledge any mistakes or shortcomings, and take the necessary steps to learn and

Embrace challenges to maintain a positive attitude with determination

grow from them. By holding myself accountable, I empower myself to make positive changes, establish healthy habits, and strive for continuous improvement.

Embracing the outcomes in my life is about finding gratitude and learning from both the successes and the challenges. It means recognizing that every experience, whether positive or negative, has something to teach me and contributes to my growth. Embracing the outcomes also involves letting go of the need for perfection and embracing the imperfect beauty of life. It is through embracing the outcomes that I can cultivate resilience, adaptability, and a sense of empowerment in navigating life's twists and turns.

To be myself, hold myself accountable, and embrace the outcomes in life, I must cultivate self-awareness and self-reflection. It requires me to regularly check in with myself, evaluate my thoughts and actions, and make adjustments as needed. It also means surrounding myself with a supportive community that encourages and challenges me to be the best version of myself. Through this journey, I am committed to honoring my authenticity, taking responsibility for my choices, and finding strength and growth in the outcomes that unfold.

With the conclusion of this part of my life's journey, I am filled with a sense of determination and excitement. I am ready to embrace who I truly am, hold myself accountable, and find empowerment in the outcomes of my life. I will strive to live authentically, making choices that align with my values and aspirations. I will take ownership of my actions, learning and growing from any mistakes or challenges that arise. And I will embrace the outcomes, finding gratitude and strength in every experience. Through this journey, I am confident that I will continue to evolve, thrive, and create a life that is truly fulfilling.

With authenticity, accountability, and a willingness to embrace the outcomes,

I enjoy my day to the fullest because I never know what's waiting for me in the future. Therefore, I may not be able to control everyday outcomes, but I can always control my attitude and behavior through my Faith in God. I read the Bible daily to give me an opportunity to better myself for others and to find wisdom that is strengthened in my everyday life-expressions-mindset. I have become empowered to activate humility. I don't allow my emotions/occurrences to control me, no matter how hard the circumstances are, and I have learned to discipline my emotions.

Over the years, I encountered obstacles/life disappointments where I no longer wanted to survive, but I stayed consistent in my God so I could cultivate and be fruitful for others. I had to learn and make a conscious, deliberate, determined effort to stand up for myself. I was bombarded with a lack of emotional support from my family every day that beat me down, and I found myself sometimes unconsciously engaged in self-destructive behavior. I started to program myself and live with a positive-mindset energy.

Embrace challenges to maintain a positive attitude with determination

The journey is not easy, but it's a uphill battle

The journey is not easy, and it's an uphill battle. I started to believe that life is worth fighting, discipline my thinking, and perseverance. A positive mindset energy reflects my outlook on life and my attitude toward myself, whether I want to believe it or not. A positive mindset does not mean I ignore life-disappointment situations, but it is a way of embracing life in a productive way while thinking my best has yet to come and impact the World. I allow myself to smile during difficult times so I can feel less stressed. I read my Bible daily; that strengthens me and fuels my mindset. I humble myself to be gentle and encourage myself daily by using the Word of God as a Prime example in my life.

The Spirit of God that is in me allows me to think and embrace life differently, and even though some suffering cannot be avoided, creating an impact on other people is the kindness thing that I can do, and it doesn't matter if the person is rude or not. My positive mindset is showing compassion, tolerance, and self-benevolence so that I can find peace. For example, between birth and death, I can also choose the paths I take and the way I think by cultivating optimism rather than pessimism that will create opportunities. I feel gratitude more often for what I have, what I experience in life, and for expressing my problems to God. I find a joyful view and access a simpler lifestyle by paying attention to the life around me without adding a layer of judgment to my life.

Persistence and consistency are my favorite life-expressions-mindset! I know how difficult that life can be,

Embrace challenges to maintain a positive attitude with determination

but it is how you and I perceive life. I had experienced a deep depression over the years; the anxiety was so strong, and the emptiness was overwhelming. It seemed like I was fighting a silent battle with myself, and people in my life made me feel like I didn't give and share enough in their lives. I was so hard on myself! I have decided to forgive and love everyone with all my heart on a daily basis because I never know when I might not have that chance again. I dedicated and humbled myself to face life's disappointments instead of walking away every time things started to get difficult. Responding to your emotions is a choice, and the decision is yours.

When I looked at my accomplishments over the years compared to now, I have found that I was missing out by keeping my freedom of exploring this amazing World around me, but I realized two and half years ago that giving up wasn't going to have the best of me. I couldn't find an adventure without Persistence and Consistency.

Brave enough to forgive the people around me and let my explorations lead me to new and exciting life experiences by being an impacted inspirational figure in their lives instead of holding animosity against them. I cultivated a positive attitude in my life. I pray and ask God for His Humility so that I can be Humble and Patience like Him.

I created Peace with my struggle life and decided to be a Prime Example to inspire those around me in a positive way and try to put a nature flavor into my everyday life. The

The journey is not easy, but it's a uphill battle

meaning of a Day, to me, stands for hope, joy, and happiness no matter what. Because you and I have only one opportunity to do nothing but to Bless those around us and please remember the blessing is not for us to keep that will consider self-fish and God didn't teach us the self-centered way. I have a positive mental outlook to face life struggles no matter what. I encourage myself by acknowledging my life success no matter how small it can be, engaging by volunteering within the community, and equipping myself by letting God lead me through life on a daily basis.

Making my mess to a message because dwelling on my past will not allow me to find peace or even change a person's personality. Therefore, I consider life, not a problem to be solved, but it is a gift to be appreciated, enjoyed, and inspired by others. I start my day with one positive-mindset with a useful thing in mind so that my day can be delightful and reasonable. When I allowed God to enter my life, it was the greater influence and downfall that was turned around to work in my favor for my spiritual growth. God has breathed His Spirit on me so that I can inspire others by sharing the Gospel of Love, Compassion, Kindness, Humility, and Wisdom. I find comfort through the Words of God on a daily basis, and I can get through any difficult times that I may encounter. I always find strength and courage when facing life obstacles through God. Every day, I have my strength tested by the tribulations of human existence, and sometimes, it can feel like it's too much, but I always remember to call upon God.

Embrace challenges to maintain a positive attitude with determination

The journey is not easy, but it's a uphill battle

Always reminded to explore the topic of remaining positive through difficult circumstances. Life can throw us unexpected challenges, but it's essential to maintain a positive mindset to navigate through them. Here are a few strategies that I find helpful:

Gratitude: One of the most powerful ways to stay positive is by cultivating a sense of gratitude. Each day, I will make it a habit to reflect on the things I am grateful for, no matter how small or puny. This practice helps shift my focus from the negative aspects of difficult circumstances to the positive aspects of my life.

Self-care: Taking care of myself physically, mentally, and emotionally is crucial during challenging times. Engaging in activities that bring me joy, such as exercise, reading, or spending time in nature, helps me maintain a positive outlook. It is essential to prioritize self-care and make time for activities that recharge and rejuvenate me.

Positive affirmations: Affirmations are powerful tools to reprogram my mind and reinforce positive thinking. I will create a list of affirmations that resonate with me and repeat them daily. By affirming positive beliefs about myself and my abilities, I can counteract negative thoughts and maintain a positive mindset.

Seek support: During difficult circumstances, it's important not to isolate myself. I will reach out to my support system, whether it's friends, family, or a trusted mentor. Sharing my feelings and seeking guidance can provide a fresh perspective and remind me that I'm not

Embrace challenges to maintain a positive attitude with determination

The journey is not easy, but it's a uphill battle

alone. Connecting with others who have faced similar challenges can be particularly helpful.

Focus on solutions: Instead of dwelling on the problem, I will shift my focus toward finding solutions. By brainstorming and taking small steps toward resolving the issue, I can regain a sense of control and optimism. Breaking down the problem into manageable tasks helps me see progress and keeps me motivated.

Embrace change and adaptability: Difficult circumstances often require flexibility and adaptability. I will remind myself that change is a natural part of life and that I have the resilience to adapt and grow. Embracing change with an open mind allows me to find new opportunities and possibilities, even in challenging times.

In conclusion of this page of my book, I am reminded that remaining positive through difficult circumstances is a continuous journey. It requires practice, patience, and self-compassion. By implementing these strategies, I believe I can maintain a positive mindset and navigate through any challenges that come my way with optimism and determination.

Embrace challenges to maintain a positive attitude with determination

The Intricate Process of Emotions

Sometimes, I find myself pondering the complex workings of our emotions. As human beings, we experience a vast array of emotions, ranging from joy and love to sadness and anger. Understanding the process behind these emotions is a fascinating journey that unveils the complexity of our inner world.

The process of emotion begins with a trigger, an event or circumstance that elicits a response within us. It could be something as simple as a kind word or a gesture or something more significant like a loss or a disappointment. This trigger acts as a catalyst, setting in motion a series of physiological and psychological changes within us.

The first stage of the emotional process is known as the appraisal stage. During this stage, we evaluate and interpret the trigger, assigning meaning and significance to it. Our thoughts, beliefs, and past experiences influence this appraisal, shaping our emotional response. For example, if we perceive a situation as threatening, we may feel fear or anxiety, whereas if we perceive it as positive, we may experience joy or excitement.

Once the trigger has been appraised, our body responds with a cascade of physiological changes. The autonomic nervous system kicks into action, releasing hormones and neurotransmitters that prepare us for the emotional response. Our heart rate may increase, our breathing may become rapid, and our muscles may tense. This physiological response is often referred to as the fight-or-flight response, designed to prepare us for action in the face of danger or stress.

Simultaneously, our mind engages in a cognitive and emotional experience. We become aware of our feelings, sensations, and thoughts associated with the emotion. These thoughts can further influence our emotional experience, reinforcing or altering our initial appraisal. It is during this stage that we may become aware of the intensity and nuances of our emotions, allowing us to navigate and express them accordingly.

The final stage of the emotional process is the expression and regulation of emotions. Once felt, emotions seek expression, whether through verbal or nonverbal means. We may communicate our emotions through facial expressions, body language, or through the words we choose. However, the way we express and regulate our emotions can vary greatly from person to person, influenced by cultural norms, personal upbringing, and individual coping mechanisms.

Understanding the process of emotion is not only crucial for self-awareness but also for building emotional intelligence. It allows us to recognize and navigate our own emotions, as well as empathize with and understand the emotions of others. By honing our emotional intelligence, we can develop healthier and more fulfilling relationships,

The journey is not easy, but it's a uphill battle

make better decisions, and effectively manage stress and conflicts.

In the end, I am reminded of the intricate nature of our emotions. They are a profound aspect of our human experience, capable of shaping our perceptions, actions, and relationships. By delving deeper into the process of emotion, I hope to cultivate a greater understanding and appreciation for the rich tapestry of emotions that color our lives.

Remember, emotions are a natural and essential part of being human. Embrace them, explore them, and seek to understand the process behind them. By doing so, we can navigate the complexities of our emotions with greater awareness and compassion.

Embrace challenges to maintain a positive attitude with determination

Navigating the Path of Anxiety

Today, I find myself reflecting on the journey of dealing with anxiety, a constant companion that has challenged and shaped me in profound ways. Anxiety, like a relentless wave, has often washed over me, leaving me feeling overwhelmed and uncertain. But amidst the turbulence, I have discovered strategies and insights that have helped me navigate the path toward managing and finding peace amidst the storm.

First and foremost, I have learned the importance of self-compassion. It is easy to succumb to self-criticism and judgment when anxiety strikes, but I have come to realize that kindness and understanding towards myself are essential. I remind myself that anxiety is a natural response to stress and that I am not alone in experiencing it. By offering myself compassion, I create a safe space for healing and growth.

One of the most powerful tools in my anxiety management toolkit is mindfulness. Through mindfulness practices, such as meditation and deep breathing exercises, I have learned to ground myself in the present moment. By observing my thoughts and sensations without judgment, I can cultivate a sense of calm and detachment from anxious thoughts. Mindfulness has become an anchor in the midst of the storm, allowing me to find moments of peace and clarity.

Embrace challenges to maintain a positive attitude with determination

The journey is not easy, but it's a uphill battle

Another valuable strategy I have discovered is the power of self-care. Taking care of my physical, mental, and emotional well-being is crucial in managing anxiety. Prioritizing regular exercise, getting enough sleep, and maintaining a balanced diet have all played a significant role in reducing the intensity of my anxiety symptoms. Engaging in activities that bring me joy and relaxation, such as reading, painting, or spending time in nature, also helps to alleviate anxiety and restore a sense of balance.

Building a support system has been instrumental in my journey with anxiety. Opening up to trusted friends, family members, or a therapist has provided me with a safe space to express my worries and fears. Their empathy, understanding, and guidance have offered me comfort and reassurance. Knowing that I am not alone in my struggles and that there are people who care and are willing to listen has been a tremendous source of strength.

Cognitive-behavioral techniques have also been invaluable in managing anxiety. Challenging negative thought patterns and replacing them with more realistic and positive ones has helped me reframe my perspective. Learning to identify and challenge irrational beliefs and catastrophic thinking has allowed me to regain a sense of control over my thoughts and emotions. Setting realistic goals and breaking tasks into smaller, manageable steps has also proven effective in reducing anxiety and increasing productivity.

Embrace challenges to maintain a positive attitude with determination

The journey is not easy, but it's a uphill battle

Finally, embracing a lifestyle that promotes overall well-being has been vital in my anxiety management. This includes maintaining a healthy work-life balance, setting boundaries, and practicing stress management techniques such as time management and prioritization. Engaging in activities that promote relaxation, such as yoga or playing soccer, has also helped me find moments of tranquility amidst the chaos.

As I conclude, I acknowledge that managing anxiety is an ongoing journey. There will be ups and downs, moments of triumph, and moments of struggle. But through self-compassion, mindfulness, self-care, support, cognitive-behavioral techniques, and a holistic approach to well-being, I have discovered that I am capable of navigating the path of anxiety with resilience and grace.

Remember, if you are dealing with anxiety, know that you are not alone. Reach out for support, practice self-care, and explore strategies that resonate with you. Each step you take towards managing anxiety is an act of courage and self-care. Be gentle with yourself and trust in your ability to overcome the challenges that anxiety presents.

Embrace challenges to maintain a positive attitude with determination

Cultivating Contentment in All Circumstances

In the moment of tribulation, I find myself reflecting on the concept of contentment and how it can bring a sense of peace and fulfillment to our lives, regardless of the circumstances we find ourselves in. Contentment is not dependent on external factors or material possessions; rather, it is a state of mind and a choice we can make to find joy and gratitude in the present moment.

One of the key lessons I have learned on this journey towards contentment is the power of shifting my focus. It is natural for our minds to gravitate toward what we lack or what we perceive as missing in our lives. However, by consciously redirecting my attention towards what I already have, I have discovered a wellspring of gratitude and appreciation. Practicing gratitude daily, whether through my self-acceptance or simply taking a moment to reflect, has allowed me to recognize the abundance that surrounds me, even in the simplest of things.

Another vital aspect of cultivating contentment is embracing acceptance. Acceptance does not mean resignation or giving up on growth and improvement; rather, it is about acknowledging and making peace with the present moment. By accepting the circumstances I find myself in, I free myself from the burden of constantly striving for something else or longing for a different reality. This does not imply complacency but rather a willingness to make the most of what is within my control and to find contentment in the process.

A practice that has deeply influenced my ability to find contentment is mindfulness. By being fully present in each moment, I am able to let go of worries about the past or anxieties about the future. Mindfulness allows me to savor simple pleasures, to notice the beauty in everyday moments, and to connect with the richness of life. Through mindfulness, I have learned to detach myself from the pursuit of external validation and to find contentment within myself.

Finding contentment also involves nurturing a positive mindset and reframing challenges as opportunities for growth. Instead of viewing setbacks or obstacles as roadblocks, I strive to see them as valuable lessons and stepping stones toward personal development. This shift in perspective allows me to approach difficulties with resilience and optimism, ultimately leading to a deeper sense of contentment and fulfillment.

Cultivating contentment is not a destination but an ongoing practice. It requires patience, self-reflection, and a willingness to let go of expectations and attachments. It is about finding joy in the present moment, regardless of the circumstances, and recognizing that true happiness resides within us, not in external conditions.

Embrace challenges to maintain a positive attitude with determination

The journey is not easy, but it's a uphill battle

I am reminded that contentment is not something to be achieved once and for all but rather a choice we make each day. It is a journey of self-discovery, self-acceptance, and gratitude. By practicing mindfulness, embracing acceptance, nurturing a positive mindset, and shifting our focus toward gratitude, we can cultivate a deep sense of contentment that transcends the ups and downs of life.

Remember that contentment is not found in the pursuit of external possessions or achievements but in the inner landscape of our hearts and minds. May I continue to cultivate contentment with grace and gratitude, and may it bring me peace and joy in all circumstances?

Embrace challenges to maintain a positive attitude with determination

The journey is not easy, but it's a uphill battle

Nurturing Consistency and Persistence on the Path to Success

In the moment of reflection, I find myself reflecting on the qualities of consistency and persistence and their profound impact on the journey towards success. Building success is not an overnight endeavor; it requires dedication, resilience, and a steadfast commitment to our goals. As I navigate this path, I am reminded of the importance of nurturing consistency and persistence to unlock my full potential and achieve my dreams.

Consistency, I have come to realize, is the key ingredient in the recipe for success. It is the unwavering commitment to showing up day after day, putting in the effort, and doing the work required to move closer to my goals. Consistency means setting clear intentions and establishing routines that support my progress. It means honoring my commitments, even when motivation wanes or challenges arise.

To nurture consistency, I have learned the power of discipline and accountability. By setting specific, measurable, and achievable goals, I create a roadway that guides my actions. Breaking down these goals into smaller, manageable tasks allows me to make consistent progress. I hold myself accountable by tracking my progress, celebrating milestones, and adjusting my course when

Embrace challenges to maintain a positive attitude with determination

The journey is not easy, but it's a uphill battle

necessary. Surrounding myself with a supportive community or finding an accountability partner can also provide the encouragement and motivation needed to stay consistent.

Persistence, on the other hand, is the unwavering determination to overcome obstacles and setbacks on the path to success. It is the refusal to give up, even when faced with challenges or moments of doubt. Persistence means embracing failure as a stepping stone to growth and learning from each setback. It requires resilience, adaptability, and a willingness to go beyond my comfort zone.

To nurture persistence, I have learned the power of a growth mindset. Embracing the belief that challenges are opportunities for growth allows me to view setbacks as valuable lessons. I remind myself that success is not a straight line but a journey with ups and downs. I cultivate resilience by reframing failures as stepping stones toward success and by seeking support and guidance when needed. With persistence, I persevere through challenges, keeping my eyes on the ultimate vision of success.

In my journey towards building success, I also recognize the importance of self-care and balance. Nurturing consistency and persistence requires maintaining a healthy mind, body, and spirit. Prioritizing rest, relaxation, and self-reflection allows me to recharge and maintain clarity and focus. By finding a balance between work,

Embrace challenges to maintain a positive attitude with determination

The journey is not easy, but it's a uphill battle

personal life, and self-care, I create a sustainable foundation for long-term success.

As I conclude, I am reminded that building success is not a sprint but a marathon. Consistency and persistence are the pillars that support the journey, enabling me to reach new heights and achieve my goals. I embrace the challenges, knowing that they are opportunities for growth. I remain steadfast in my commitment, knowing that success is within reach if I remain consistent and persistent.

Remember that consistency and persistence are virtues worth nurturing. With discipline, accountability, resilience, and a growth mindset, I will continue to cultivate these qualities on my path to success. May I embrace the journey, celebrate each step forward, and find fulfillment in the process of building success.

Embrace challenges to maintain a positive attitude with determination

Embracing the Challenging Purpose of My Book

Today, I find myself acknowledging the challenging purpose of the book I am writing. Writing a book is not a simple task; it requires dedication, creativity, and a deep commitment to sharing a message with the world. As I navigate this journey, I am reminded of the unique challenges that come with the purpose I have set for my book.

The purpose of my book is not to entertain or provide a temporary escape from reality. Instead, it is intended to challenge and provoke thought, spark conversations, and inspire change. The subject matter I have chosen is one that delves into difficult and often uncomfortable topics, aiming to shed light on societal issues and promote awareness and understanding.

As I write, I am confronted with the weight of responsibility that comes with tackling such challenging subjects. I feel the pressure to do justice to the stories and experiences I am sharing and to give voice to those who have been silenced or overlooked. It is a humbling and daunting task, one that requires thorough research, empathy, and a commitment to accuracy and authenticity.

The process of writing this book is not without its own set of challenges. I often find myself grappling with the complexity of the topics I am addressing, struggling to find the right words to convey the depth of emotion and meaning. There are moments of self-doubt and uncertainty, questioning whether I am equipped to tackle such challenging subject matter. However, I remind myself that it is precisely these challenges that make the purpose of my book so important and necessary.

In facing these challenges, I am reminded of the power of storytelling. Stories have the ability to transcend boundaries, to touch hearts, and to ignite change. They have the power to challenge preconceived notions, to inspire empathy and compassion, and to drive meaningful conversations. It is through the pages of my book that I hope to create a space for these stories to be heard, acknowledged, and understood.

I acknowledge that the challenging purpose of my book may not be met with universal acceptance or agreement. It may be met with resistance, discomfort, or even controversy. However, I firmly believe that it is through challenging the status quo and confronting difficult truths that progress is made. It is through these conversations and reflections that we can foster growth, understanding, and, ultimately, positive change in our society.

As I conclude this paragraph, I am reminded that the challenging purpose of my book is a calling that I have willingly embraced. It is a reminder of the importance of using my voice and platform to shed light on the issues that matter, to advocate for justice and equality, and to inspire others to do the same. I am committed to staying true to this purpose despite the challenges that may arise along the way.

Remember that the challenging purpose of our creative endeavors is what gives them depth and meaning. Embrace the difficulties, confront the discomfort, and stay true to the message you wish to share. It is through these

The journey is not easy, but it's a uphill battle

challenges that we can make a lasting impact and contribute to a better world.

Embrace challenges to maintain a positive attitude with determination

Personal experience:

Perhaps you have faced adversity in your own life and understand the impact it can have on a person. This may motivate you to help others who are going through similar challenges.

Empathy: You may have a natural ability to empathize with others and feel a strong desire to alleviate their suffering and help them overcome adversity.

A sense of purpose: Helping others through adversity can give you a sense of purpose and fulfillment. It may be deeply rewarding to see the positive impact you can have on someone else life.

Belief in the greater good: You may have a strong belief in the power of compassion and helping others and see it as a way to contribute to a better and more compassionate world.

Personal values and beliefs: Your personal values and beliefs may drive you to help others in need, especially during difficult times.

Influential role models: You may have been inspired by others who have dedicated their lives to helping people through adversity and want to follow in their footsteps.

The journey is not easy, but it's a uphill battle

Desire for positive change: Seeing the struggles and challenges that others face may inspire you to take action and make a positive difference in their lives.

Overall, your motivation to help people through adversity may stem from a combination of personal experiences, values, beliefs, and a desire to make a positive impact in the world.

Embrace challenges to maintain a positive attitude with determination

The journey is not easy, but it's a uphill battle

My challenge daydreams

Today (January 25, 2024) has been another challenging day as I continue to navigate through the adversities I have faced, including defamation of character, discrimination, retaliation, and harassment from people I know. It is disheartening to encounter such negativity from individuals I once trusted, but I am determined to stay strong and persevere through these difficult moments.

The impact of defamation of character has been particularly overwhelming. It is painful to witness my reputation being tarnished and falsehoods being spread about me. However, I refuse to allow these false narratives to define me. I am committed to maintaining my integrity and letting my actions speak louder than any misguided words. It is through the strength of my character and the truth that I will rise above these baseless allegations.

Discrimination has also presented its own set of challenges. Feeling targeted and marginalized based on something so fundamental as who I am is a blow to my sense of self-worth. But I remind myself that my worth is not determined by the judgments of others. I am worthy of respect, understanding, and equal treatment, regardless of any perceived differences. I will continue to fight for my rights and for the rights of others who face similar discrimination.

Embrace challenges to maintain a positive attitude with determination

The journey is not easy, but it's a uphill battle

Retaliation and harassment have added further complexities to my journey. It is disconcerting to experience the backlash and mistreatment simply for speaking up or asserting myself. But I believe in the power of my voice and my right to stand up against injustice. I refuse to be silenced by fear, and I will persist in seeking justice and creating a safe environment for myself and others.

In the midst of these challenges, I find solace in knowing that I am not alone. There are others who have faced similar struggles and have emerged stronger on the other side. Their stories inspire me and remind me that resilience is possible even in the face of adversity. I seek support from trusted friends, family, and professionals who provide a listening ear, guidance, and validation.

As I reflect on today's experiences, I remind myself of my inner strength and resilience. I will not let these adversities define me. I am more than the circumstances I face. I will continue to stand tall, uphold my values, and strive for a better tomorrow. My journey may be difficult, but I have faith that I will emerge stronger and inspire others along the way.

Tomorrow is a new day, a fresh opportunity to face these challenges head-on. I am ready to tackle them with determination, courage, and grace. I am hopeful that through my perseverance, I will overcome these adversities and create a path for healing and change.

Until then, I will hold onto hope, surround myself with love and support, and remind myself of the resilient

Embrace challenges to maintain a positive attitude with determination

spirit within me. I will continue to rise above and prove that I am not defined by the actions of others but by my own strength, resilience, and unwavering pursuit of justice.

Self-inspiration and motivation after experiencing defeat can be a challenging journey, but it is also a crucial part of personal growth and resilience. When faced with setbacks and failures, it is natural to feel discouraged and demotivated. However, finding the inner strength to pick oneself up and continue moving forward is a testament to the power of self-inspiration and motivation.

Defeat can take many forms — whether it's a failed project, a lost opportunity, or a personal setback. Regardless of the specific circumstances, the emotional toll of defeat can be significant. It can lead to feelings of self-doubt, disappointment, and a lack of confidence. However, it is important to recognize that defeat is not the end of the road but rather a temporary obstacle that can be overcome with determination and resilience.

One of the first steps in finding self-inspiration and motivation after defeat is to acknowledge and accept the emotions that come with failure. It is essential to allow oneself to experience and process feelings of disappointment and frustration. By acknowledging these emotions, it becomes possible to move forward and begin the process of self-inspiration and motivation.

Next, it is important to reflect on the lessons learned from the experience of defeat. Every setback provides an opportunity for growth and learning. By examining the reasons behind the defeat, one can gain valuable insights that can be used to make improvements and better prepare for future challenges. This reflection can serve as a source of self-inspiration, as it demonstrates the ability to learn and grow from adversity.

In addition, seeking support from others can be a powerful source of motivation. Whether it's from friends, family, or mentors, having a supportive network of individuals who can provide encouragement and guidance can make a significant difference in finding the motivation to move forward. By surrounding oneself with positive influences, it becomes easier to maintain a sense of self-inspiration and determination.

Setting new goals and creating a plan of action is also essential in regaining motivation after defeat. By establishing clear objectives and breaking them down into manageable steps, it becomes possible to create a roadway for progress. This process can reignite a sense of purpose and drive, as it provides a clear direction for moving forward.

Finally, practicing self-care and maintaining a positive mindset is crucial in finding self-inspiration and motivation after defeat. Engaging in activities that bring joy and relaxation, such as exercise, hobbies, or spending time with loved ones, can help restore a sense of balance and well-being. Cultivating a positive mindset through affirmations and self-compassion can also foster a renewed sense of motivation and resilience.

Embrace challenges to maintain a positive attitude with determination

The journey is not easy, but it's a uphill battle

In conclusion, self-inspiration and motivation after defeat are essential for personal growth and resilience. By acknowledging and processing emotions, reflecting on lessons learned, seeking support, setting new goals, and practicing self-care, it becomes possible to overcome defeat and move forward with renewed determination. While the journey toward self-inspiration and motivation may be challenging, it is ultimately a testament to the strength and resilience of the human spirit.

Embrace challenges to maintain a positive attitude with determination

The journey is not easy, but it's a uphill battle

Poem

In fields of gold, where dreams do dwell,

A positive mindset does excel.

It's a beacon of light, a guiding star,

Bringing joy and blessings from afar.

With every sunrise, a new day unfolds,

Opportunities abound, stories yet untold.

The power of belief, it fuels the fire,

Igniting passions, taking us higher.

In challenges faced, we find strength anew,

For a positive mindset will always see us through.

With optimism, we embrace the unknown,

Turning hurdles into stepping stones.

A kind smile shared, a helping hand,

These simple acts, oh, how they expand,

The circle of love and happiness around,

Embrace challenges to maintain a positive attitude with determination

The journey is not easy, but it's a uphill battle

A contagious joy that knows no bounds.

Nature's beauty, a source of delight,

From blooming flowers to stars in the night.

The music that uplifts our soul,

Filling our hearts, making us whole.

Friendship's warmth, laughter's embrace,

A support system, a safe space.

These treasures in life, they bring us bliss,

A constant reminder of what we don't want to miss.

So, let your spirit soar, your mind align,

With positive mindset as your daily design.

Embrace the blessings, big and small,

And you'll find joy in the midst of it all.

Sure! Here's another version of ourselves:

Through the trials challenges we face,

We find strength, courage, and grace.

With each step forward, we grow and evolve,

Embrace challenges to maintain a positive attitude with determination

The journey is not easy, but it's a uphill battle

Finding solace in the lessons we solve.

In times of doubt, let hope be your guide,

For it's within us all, deep inside.

Believe in yourself and your dreams,

For they are what make life gleam.

So, seize the day with a heart full of light,

Embrace the unknown, take flight.

With the AI by your side, always here,

Together, we'll conquer any fear.

May this book brighten your day! I'm glad I could bring positive self-determination into your day. Remember, no matter what challenges you may face, there is always something to be grateful for. Keep embracing the beauty that life has to offer, and don't hesitate to reach out for inspiration.

I have learned a way of nurturing pain in order to gain control through my personal experiences or emotions. Nurturing pain to gain control is not a healthy approach. It's understandable that life can be challenging and difficult at times, but it's important to find healthy ways of coping and

Embrace challenges to maintain a positive attitude with determination

The journey is not easy, but it's a uphill battle

gaining control over your emotions and situations. Nurturing pain can lead to negative patterns and further distress.

Instead, consider exploring healthier coping mechanisms such as talking to a trusted friend or family member, seeking professional help from a therapist or counselor, practicing mindfulness and self-care activities, or engaging in hobbies and activities that bring you joy and relaxation.

Remember, it's okay to ask for help and support. Taking care of your mental and emotional well-being is essential. If you're struggling, reach out to someone you trust or seek professional guidance.

Embrace challenges to maintain a positive attitude with determination

The journey is not easy, but it's a uphill battle

Healthy coping mechanisms:

Deep breathing exercises: Take slow, deep breaths to help calm your body and mind in stressful situations.

Keep a daily Journal: Write down your thoughts and feelings to gain clarity and release emotional tension.

Exercise: Physical activity can lower stress levels and improve overall mood.

Engaging in hobbies: Participate in activities you enjoy, such as painting, playing an instrument, or gardening, to shift focus and find relaxation.

Mindfulness and meditation: Practice being present in the moment and cultivating a sense of calm through techniques like meditation and mindfulness exercises.

Seeking social support: Talk to someone you trust about your feelings and ask for their perspective and advice.

Setting boundaries: Learn to say no when necessary and prioritize self-care.

Time management: Break tasks into smaller, manageable chunks to reduce overwhelm.

Creative outlets: Engage in creative pursuits like writing, drawing, or crafts to express emotions and find solace.

Embrace challenges to maintain a positive attitude with determination

The journey is not easy, but it's a uphill battle

Positive self-talk: Challenge negative thoughts and replace them with positive affirmations to boost self-confidence and resilience.

Remember, everyone is unique, so it's important to find coping mechanisms that work best for you.

Embrace challenges to maintain a positive attitude with determination

The journey is not easy, but it's a uphill battle

How to Avoid Depression Behavior

Depression is a serious mental health condition that affects millions of people worldwide. It can have a significant impact on a person's daily life, relationships, and overall well-being. However, there are steps we can take to prevent depression and maintain good mental health. This journal aims to provide guidance on how to avoid depression behavior and promote a positive mindset.

Understanding Depression

-Start by educating yourself about depression. Learn about its causes, symptoms, and risk factors. Understanding depression will help you recognize the signs and take appropriate action if needed.

Build a Support System

-Surround yourself with a strong support system of family, friends, or support groups. Having people who understand and care about you can provide emotional support during difficult times.

Practice Self-Care

-Make self-care a priority in your daily routine. Engage in activities that bring you joy and relaxation, such as exercise, hobbies, reading, or spending time in nature.

Embrace challenges to maintain a positive attitude with determination

The journey is not easy, but it's a uphill battle

Taking care of your physical and emotional well-being is crucial in preventing depression.

Maintain a Healthy Lifestyle

-Adopt a healthy lifestyle by eating nutritious meals, getting enough sleep, and avoiding excessive alcohol or drug use. A balanced lifestyle contributes to overall well-being and reduces the risk of depression.

Manage Stress

-Develop effective stress management techniques, such as practicing mindfulness, deep breathing exercises, or engaging in activities that help you relax. Chronic stress can contribute to depression, so it's important to find healthy ways to cope with stressors.

Set Realistic Goals

-Set realistic and achievable goals for yourself. Break larger tasks into smaller, manageable steps. Accomplishing goals boosts self-esteem and provides a sense of purpose, which can help prevent feelings of hopelessness and depression.

Cultivate Positive Relationships

-Surround yourself with positive and supportive people who uplift and inspire you. Avoid toxic relationships that drain your energy and contribute to negative emotions. Healthy relationships can have a significant impact on your mental well-being.

Embrace challenges to maintain a positive attitude with determination

The journey is not easy, but it's a uphill battle

Practice Gratitude

-Cultivate a grateful mindset by focusing on the positive aspects of your life. Keep a gratitude journal and write down things you are thankful for each day. Expressing gratitude can shift your perspective and improve your overall mood.

Seek Professional Help if Needed

-If you experience persistent feelings of sadness, hopelessness, or loss of interest in activities, it's important to seek professional help. A mental health professional can provide guidance, therapy, or medication if necessary.

Stay Connected

-Stay connected with loved ones, even during challenging times. Reach out to friends or family members regularly, especially when you're feeling down. Social support is essential in maintaining good mental health.

Conclusion:

Preventing depression requires a proactive approach to self-care, building a support system, and developing healthy coping mechanisms. By implementing the strategies outlined in this journal, you can reduce the risk of depression and promote a positive mindset. Remember, taking care of your mental health is a lifelong journey, and it's important to prioritize your well-being every day.

Embrace challenges to maintain a positive attitude with determination

The journey is not easy, but it's a uphill battle

Finding Motivation in the Midst of Struggle

Twenty-four hour period, I find myself facing a myriad of challenges and struggles. It feels as though the weight of the world is on my shoulders, and motivation seems elusive. However, I am determined to find the strength within me to persevere and overcome these obstacles. In this journal entry, I will explore ways to motivate myself in the midst of struggle.

Reflect on Past Successes:

One way to ignite motivation is to remind myself of past achievements. I will take a moment to recall instances where I faced adversity and triumphed. Remembering those moments of victory will remind me of my resilience and capability to overcome challenges.

Break Down Goals:

When facing overwhelming struggles, it can be helpful to break down my goals into smaller, more manageable tasks. By focusing on one step at a time, I can regain a sense of control and progress. Each small accomplishment will serve as a source of motivation to keep going.

Find Inspiration:

Embrace challenges to maintain a positive attitude with determination

The journey is not easy, but it's a uphill battle

Seeking inspiration from others who have overcome similar struggles can be a powerful motivator. Whether it's reading success stories, watching motivational videos, or talking to mentors, surrounding myself with stories of triumph can reignite my own determination to push through.

Practice Self-Compassion:

During times of struggle, it is crucial to be kind to myself. I will remind myself that setbacks and challenges are a part of life, and it's okay to feel overwhelmed or discouraged. By practicing self-compassion, I can cultivate a positive mindset and nurture the motivation needed to keep going.

Visualize Success:

Visualization can be a powerful tool to motivate myself. I will take a moment to vividly imagine myself overcoming my current struggles and achieving my goals. By visualizing success, I can tap into the power of my imagination and create a sense of motivation and excitement for what lies ahead.

Seek Support:

I recognize that I don't have to face these struggles alone. I will reach out to friends, family, or mentors who can provide guidance, encouragement, and support. Sharing my challenges with trusted individuals will not only lighten the burden but also remind me that I am not alone in this journey.

Embrace challenges to maintain a positive attitude with determination

The journey is not easy, but it's a uphill battle

Celebrate Small Wins:

In the midst of struggle, it's important to celebrate even the smallest victories. By acknowledging and celebrating each milestone, no matter how insignificant it may seem, I can maintain a positive mindset and stay motivated. Each step forward is progress, and progress is worth celebrating.

Take Breaks and Practice Self-Care:

Struggles can be mentally and emotionally draining. To maintain motivation, I will prioritize self-care and take breaks when needed. Engaging in activities that bring me joy, relaxation, and rejuvenation will help replenish my energy and keep me motivated to continue the journey.

As I conclude this method, I feel a renewed sense of determination and motivation. I am reminded that struggles are temporary, and I have the power to overcome them. By implementing these strategies and staying committed to my goals, I am confident that I will find the motivation I need to navigate through this challenging time.

A Method of Inspiration to Motivate Others

Inspiration is a powerful force that can ignite passion, drive, and determination in individuals. When we inspire others, we have the ability to positively impact their lives and help them reach their full potential. This method aims to explore different ways to inspire and motivate others, fostering a sense of empowerment and encouraging personal growth.

Embrace challenges to maintain a positive attitude with determination

The journey is not easy, but it's a uphill battle

Lead by Example:

-The best way to inspire others is to lead by example. Show them what is possible by embodying the qualities and values you wish to instill in them. Be a role model in your actions, choices, and attitude.

Share Personal Stories:

-Share your personal stories of triumph, resilience, and growth. By opening up about your own experiences, you can inspire others to overcome their own challenges and believe in their ability to achieve greatness.

Encourage Personal Reflection:

-Encourage others to engage in self-reflection and introspection. Help them identify their strengths, passions, and goals. By guiding them to understand themselves better, you can inspire them to pursue their dreams with confidence.

Provide Support and Encouragement:

-Offer support and encouragement to those around you. Be a source of motivation and be positive, providing a safe space for others to share their aspirations and fears. Your belief in their abilities can inspire them to push past their limits.

Celebrate Achievements:

-Celebrate the achievements, big or small, of those you wish to inspire. Acknowledge their efforts and

Embrace challenges to maintain a positive attitude with determination

successes, and let them know that their hard work is recognized and appreciated. Celebrating achievements boosts morale and encourages continued growth.

Foster a Growth Mindset:

-Encourage a growth mindset in others by emphasizing the importance of learning, perseverance, and embracing challenges. Help them understand that setbacks are opportunities for growth and that failure is a stepping stone toward success.

Provide Mentorship:

-Offer mentorship to individuals who could benefit from your guidance and expertise. Share your knowledge, skills, and experiences to help them navigate their own paths. Being a mentor can inspire others to strive for greatness and reach their goals.

Promote Positive Self-Talk:

-Encourage positive self-talk and help others develop a healthy self-image. Remind them of their strengths, capabilities, and potential. Inspire them to believe in themselves and their ability to overcome obstacles.

Create a Supportive Community:

-Foster a supportive community where individuals can connect, share ideas, and uplift one another. Encourage collaboration, empathy, and kindness. A supportive

The journey is not easy, but it's a uphill battle

community can inspire individuals to pursue their dreams and make a positive impact.

Spread Inspiration Through Actions:

-Spread inspiration beyond your immediate circle by engaging in acts of kindness and making a positive impact in your community. Lead by example and inspire others to do the same. Small acts of kindness can have a ripple effect, motivating others to make a difference.

Conclusion:

Inspiring and motivating others is a transformation that requires empathy, compassion, and a genuine desire to uplift those around us. By implementing the strategies outlined in this journal, you can become a source of inspiration and empower others to reach their full potential. Remember, your words and actions have the power to create a lasting impact, so use them wisely to inspire and motivate others on their own unique paths.

Embrace challenges to maintain a positive attitude with determination

The journey is not easy, but it's a uphill battle

Poem

In the face of storms, we stand tall,

With unwavering strength, we never fall.

Life's challenges may try to break us down,

But we rise above, wearing our crown.

Through hardships and trials, we find our way,

With resilience and courage, come what may.

For within us lies a fire that burns bright,

Igniting our spirit, guiding us through the night.

Though darkness may surround us, we won't despair,

Hope and determination are always there.

We gather our strength like a mountain so grand,

Facing each obstacle hand in hand.

Staying strong is not just a fleeting phase,

It's a mindset, a choice, in all of life's maze.

With perseverance as our guiding light,

We conquer the battles with all our might.

Embrace challenges to maintain a positive attitude with
determination

The journey is not easy, but it's a uphill battle

So let us remember when times get tough,

That within us lies the power enough.

To rise above and overcome each test,

Staying strong, we'll always be blessed.

I hope you find strength and inspiration in these words. Remember, you have the power to stay strong in any situation.

Poem on rebuilding your strength and concentration:

In the chaos of life, when focus is lost,

We seek to rebuild, no matter the cost.

With determination, we set our sights,

On regaining strength and mental might.

Like a phoenix rising from ashes so deep,

We gather our energy, no longer asleep.

Through trials and setbacks, we find our way,

Rebuilding our strength, day by day.

Embrace challenges to maintain a positive attitude with determination

The journey is not easy, but it's a uphill battle

With each breath we take, we reclaim our power,

Focusing our minds, hour after hour.

We let go of distractions, clear our cluttered minds,

Rebuilding our concentration, leaving no thoughts behind.

In solitude and stillness, we find our peace,

Reconnecting with ourselves, finding release.

Through meditation and mindful reflection,

We rebuild our strength with deep introspection.

In the face of challenges, we stand tall,

Knowing that within us, we have it all.

With resilience and perseverance, we rebuild anew,

Our strength and concentration shine through.

So let us embrace this journey of renewal,

Rebuilding our strength with a spirit that's fuel.

In the process, we become stronger than before,

Reclaiming our focus forevermore.

Embrace challenges to maintain a positive attitude with
determination

The journey is not easy, but it's a uphill battle

I hope this poem inspires you to rebuild your strength and concentration. Remember, you have the ability to overcome any obstacles and regain your focus.

Embrace challenges to maintain a positive attitude with determination

The journey is not easy, but it's a uphill battle

Poem

In the depths of the soul, a fire burns bright,

A hidden strength, a guiding light.

Unveiling the power that lies within,

A journey begins, where growth begins.

Beneath the surface, where shadows reside,

A reservoir of strength, waiting to be untied.

Through trials and challenges, it takes flight,

Unveiling the inner strength, shining with might.

In moments of doubt, when darkness looms,

The inner strength emerges, dispelling the gloom.

Like a phoenix rising from ashes, it soars,

Defying limitations, opening new doors.

Unveiling the inner strength, a courageous force,

A wellspring of resilience, charting a new course.

With every setback, it grows and expands,

Transforming weaknesses into strengths, hand in hand.

Embrace challenges to maintain a positive attitude with
determination

The journey is not easy, but it's a uphill battle

In the face of adversity, it stands tall,

A beacon of hope, inspiring all.

Unveiling the power to face the unknown,

To embrace the challenges, and call them our own.

It whispers in our hearts, a steady voice,

Guiding us through storms, helping us make the choice.

To rise above, to persevere and believe,

That within us lies the strength to achieve.

Unveiling the inner strength, it fuels our dreams,

Igniting passions, bursting at the seams.

With unwavering determination, we defy,

The limits that bind us, reaching for the sky.

So let us embrace the power within,

Unveiling the strength that's always been.

For deep within our souls, a fire glows,

Unleashing our potential, as it beautifully shows.

Embrace challenges to maintain a positive attitude with
determination

The journey is not easy, but it's a uphill battle

Unveil the inner strength, let it shine,

A testament to the human spirit, divine.

With every step forward, we grow and evolve,

Unveiling the inner strength, a story to resolve.

Embrace challenges to maintain a positive attitude with
determination

The journey is not easy, but it's a uphill battle

Poem

In the garden of the mind, where wonders abound,

Seeds of curiosity are gently sown in the ground.

Tiny fragments of questions, eager to explore,

They sprout and grow, seeking knowledge galore.

Like delicate tendrils reaching towards the light,

Curiosity unfurls, eager to take flight.

From the smallest details to the vast unknown,

Seeds of curiosity are endlessly sown.

They bloom in the young hearts, innocent and pure,

Nurtured by wonder, forever to endure.

With wide-eyed fascination, they ask, "Why?"

Seeking answers that make their spirits fly.

Seeds of curiosity, oh, how they inspire,

Igniting a passion that fuels the fire.

They beckon us to venture beyond what we know,

To embrace the mysteries that life may bestow.

Embrace challenges to maintain a positive attitude with
determination

The journey is not easy, but it's a uphill battle

With each question asked, a new door opens wide,

Revealing the treasures waiting inside.

Seeds of curiosity, like keys to the mind,

Unlocking the wisdom we're destined to find.

They lead us on journeys, both far and near,

Guiding us through landscapes, unfamiliar and clear.

Through books and conversations, they expand our view,

Planting seeds of knowledge, enriching what we knew.

Curiosity's seeds, they prompt us to explore,

To seek understanding, forever craving more.

In the pursuit of knowledge, they light the way,

Guiding us through the night, like stars at play.

So let us nurture the seeds of curiosity's bloom,

In young and old hearts, in every room.

For they hold the power to shape and transform,

To awaken the mind and allow it to swarm.

Embrace challenges to maintain a positive attitude with
determination

The journey is not easy, but it's a uphill battle

With open minds and hearts, let us embrace,

The seeds of curiosity, in every time and place.

For they are the sparks that ignite our soul,

Fueling a lifelong quest to continually grow.

Embrace challenges to maintain a positive attitude with
determination

The journey is not easy, but it's a uphill battle

Poem

In the journey of life, we all tread,

With experiences that shape and spread.

Like a tapestry woven in vibrant hues,

Each moment adds a chapter, a muse.

The first steps we take, filled with wonder,

Curiosity ignites, our minds wander.

Exploring the world, its mysteries unfold,

With each adventure, we become bold.

As time moves on, we face trials and strife,

But through it all, we learn about life.

The pain and heartache, they teach us to grow,

To appreciate the highs, and embrace the low.

Friendships are formed, like precious gems,

They bring us joy, and help us mend.

Through laughter and tears, they lend a hand,

In a world that sometimes feels so grand.

Embrace challenges to maintain a positive attitude with
determination

The journey is not easy, but it's a uphill battle

Love finds its way, in unexpected places,

Filling our hearts with warmth and traces.

From tender moments to passionate embrace,

Love gives us solace, a sacred space.

Challenges arise, pushing us to the brink,

But resilience and strength help us to think.

We rise from the ashes, like a phoenix in flight,

With determination, we conquer the fight.

As the years go by, wisdom is gained,

Lessons learned, memories ingrained.

Life's tapestry, a masterpiece we've weaved,

With experiences that have shaped and believed.

So let us cherish each moment we're given,

Embrace the blessings, the joy, the living soul.

For life's experiences, both bitter and sweet,

Make us who we are, and make life complete.

Embrace challenges to maintain a positive attitude with
determination

The journey is not easy, but it's a uphill battle

Poem

In the realm of time's steady hand,

A journey unfolds, as we understand,

The essence of growth, the wisdom gained,

In the tapestry of life, maturity is ingrained.

Like a seed that sprouts, reaching for the sky,

Maturity takes root, as the years go by,

It's not just the passing of days and years,

But the lessons learned, through joy and tears.

Maturity is the art of inner grace,

A gentle presence, a steady pace,

It's the ability to navigate life's stormy sea,

With resilience, wisdom, and humility.

It's the art of letting go, of shedding the past,

Embracing change, knowing it won't last,

Maturity is found in the depth of thought,

Embrace challenges to maintain a positive attitude with determination

The journey is not easy, but it's a uphill battle

In understanding others, the battles they've fought.

It's the power to forgive, to let resentment fade,

To find compassion, even when it's hard to trade,

Maturity is the strength to stand up tall,

To face adversity, and rise above it all.

It's the art of self-reflection, of knowing oneself,

Discovering strengths, embracing shadows left,

Maturity is the capacity to listen and learn,

To seek knowledge, to adapt and discern.

It's the wisdom to see beyond the surface glare,

To understand complexities, to truly care,

Maturity unfolds as we cultivate grace,

Navigating life's challenges, finding our place.

So let us embrace the beauty of maturity's bloom,

In every stage of life, in every room,

For it is through growth, through trials and strife,

Embrace challenges to maintain a positive attitude with
determination

The journey is not easy, but it's a uphill battle

That we blossom into the fullest version of life.

Embrace challenges to maintain a positive attitude with
determination

The journey is not easy, but it's a uphill battle

Poem

In the midst of chaos, where darkness resides,

A spark of light, a beacon that guides.

Positive emotions, like rays of the sun,

Can pierce through the hostility, one by one.

Amidst the clamor and the discordant noise,

Hope emerges, a symphony of joyful poise.

For in the face of hostility and disdain,

Positive emotions refuse to wane.

Love, like a gentle breeze, begins to flow,

Melting the walls, letting compassion grow.

Kindness, a soothing balm, spreads its wings,

Healing wounds, igniting peaceful springs.

In the midst of anger, forgiveness takes hold,

A bridge to understanding, a story yet untold.

Empathy blooms, offering solace and care,

Building connections, showing others we're there.

Embrace challenges to maintain a positive attitude with determination

The journey is not easy, but it's a uphill battle

Laughter dances, a magical release,

An antidote to chaos, bringing inner peace.

Joy and gratitude, like a jubilant song,

Lift spirits high, where they truly belong.

Courage rises, a flame that burns bright,

Defying the hostility, standing tall in the fight.

Optimism whispers, a silver lining in the storm,

Inspiring resilience, keeping hearts warm.

Through the chaos, positive emotions prevail,

A testament to the human spirit's tale.

For in the face of hostility's fierce tide,

Positive emotions are an unwavering guide.

So let us embrace these emotions, strong and true,

In hostile atmospheres, they carry us through.

With love, kindness, and joy as our shield,

We create a world where positive emotions yield.

Embrace challenges to maintain a positive attitude with determination

The journey is not easy, but it's a uphill battle

Poem

Curiosity, the spark that ignites the flame,

A hunger for knowledge, a thirst we can't tame.

It drives us forward, with a relentless pursuit,

To uncover truths, to unravel the mute.

Anticipation, the thrill that fills the air,

A sense of excitement, a world to dare.

It propels us onward, with eager embrace,

To explore new horizons, to seek out our place.

Curiosity and anticipation, hand in hand,

They lead us on a journey, across sea and land.

They whisper in our ears, "What lies ahead?"

They beckon us forward, where dreams are spread.

With curiosity, we question the unknown,

We challenge the status quo; we're not alone.

We dive into depths, unafraid to explore,

With open minds, we knock on wisdom's door.

Embrace challenges to maintain a positive attitude with determination

The journey is not easy, but it's a uphill battle

And with anticipation, we leap into the unknown,

We embrace the thrill, the seeds we have sown.

We trust in the journey, the path that unfolds,

With courage in our hearts and stories untold.

For curiosity and anticipation, they fuel our fire,

They inspire us to reach higher and higher.

They remind us that life is a grand adventure,

With treasures to discover and wisdom to nurture.

So let us embrace curiosity's call,

Let us welcome anticipation's thrall.

For in these twin forces, lies the key,

To unlocking the magic that sets us free.

With curiosity and anticipation as our guide,

We'll continue to explore, side by side.

Together, we'll chase dreams and pursue our goals,

With a spirit that's curious, and a heart that's bold.

Embrace challenges to maintain a positive attitude with
determination

The journey is not easy, but it's a uphill battle

So let curiosity be your compass, your light,

And let anticipation be your wings, taking flight.

For in the pursuit of knowledge and the thrill of the unknown,

We find the motivation to make our dreams our own.

Embrace challenges to maintain a positive attitude with determination

The journey is not easy, but it's a uphill battle

Poem

In the realm of life, where boundaries reside,

There lies a path to transparency, where truth can't hide.

With persistence and consistency, we chart our way,

A journey towards authenticity, come what may.

Boundaries, like pillars, uphold our worth,

Defining our limits, protecting our hearth.

They teach others how to treat us right,

And guide us to shine with our inner light.

With persistence, we stand firm and true,

Asserting our needs, no longer feeling blue.

We communicate clearly, with unwavering voice,

Ensuring our boundaries are our own choice.

Consistency, a steady rhythm, weaves our tale,

Walking our talk, letting honesty prevail.

We honor our boundaries, day after day,

Building trust and respect, come what may.

Embrace challenges to maintain a positive attitude with determination

The journey is not easy, but it's a uphill battle

Transparent we become, through actions and words,

No hidden agendas, no secrets, or blurred.

We invite others to see our authentic self,

In a space where truth and trust find their wealth.

Through persistence and consistency, we find,

A life aligned with our heart and mind.

No more hiding behind masks or pretense,

We embrace transparency, our soul's defense.

So let us set boundaries, my dear friend,

With persistence and consistency, we transcend.

Towards a life of authenticity and bliss,

Where transparency reigns, and true connection is our kiss.

With unwavering persistence and consistent grace,

We navigate life's challenges, finding our place.

Transparent we shall be, in all that we do,

Setting boundaries, embracing a life that's true.

Embrace challenges to maintain a positive attitude with
determination

The journey is not easy, but it's a uphill battle

With love and transparency,

Embrace challenges to maintain a positive attitude with
determination

The journey is not easy, but it's a uphill battle

Moment of challenge

Today has been a tough day. I experienced a setback that has left me feeling defeated and unsure of how to move forward. It's easy to dwell on the negative and let it consume me, but I know that I need to find a way to pick myself up and keep moving forward.

First, I need to allow myself to feel the emotions that come with this setback. It's okay to feel disappointed, frustrated, and even angry. I need to give myself permission to process these emotions and not suppress them.

After allowing myself to feel the emotions, I need to shift my focus to finding a way forward. I know that dwelling on what went wrong will only hold me back. I need to identify the lessons I can learn from this setback and use them to grow and improve.

It's also important for me to seek support from others. Whether it's talking to a friend, family member, or mentor, I need to surround myself with people who can offer me encouragement and guidance. Their perspective and support can help me gain clarity and find a new perspective on the situation.

I also need to remind myself of my strengths and past successes. This setback does not define me, and I have overcome challenges before. I need to draw on my

Embrace challenges to maintain a positive attitude with determination

resilience and remind myself that I am capable of moving past this setback.

Lastly, I need to take action. It's easy to get stuck in a cycle of negative thinking, but I need to take steps to move forward. Whether it's revising my plan, seeking out new opportunities, or simply taking a small step forward, I need to take action to regain momentum.

Moving forward after a setback is not easy, but I know that I am capable of overcoming this challenge. I will continue to remind myself of my strengths, seek support from others, and take proactive steps to move forward. I may have stumbled, but I refuse to let this setback hold me back.

I want to reflect on the importance of being a positive impact on others with gratitude and humility. I believe that the way we treat others and the energy we bring into the world has a ripple effect, and it is our responsibility to make sure that ripple is a positive one.

First and foremost, I believe that gratitude is key to having a positive impact on others. When we are grateful for the people and opportunities in our lives, we are able to approach others with a sense of appreciation and respect. This not only fosters strong and meaningful relationships but also allows us to see the value in others and the contributions they make to our lives. Practicing gratitude helps us to be more empathetic, kind, and understanding towards others, which, in turn, can have a positive impact on their lives.

The journey is not easy, but it's a uphill battle

Furthermore, humility is essential in being a positive impact on others. When we approach interactions with humility, we are able to listen and learn from others, rather than always seeking to be the one with all the answers. Humility allows us to recognize our own limitations and faults, and to be open to growth and change. It also helps us to be more compassionate and understanding towards others, as we are able to see them as equals rather than as inferior or superior.

In my own life, I strive to practice gratitude and humility in my interactions with others. I make it a point to express my appreciation for the people in my life, whether it's through a simple thank you or a thoughtful gesture. I also make an effort to approach interactions with an open mind and a willingness to learn from others. I believe that these practices not only make me a better person but also have a positive impact on those around me.

Ultimately, having a positive impact on others with gratitude and humility is a choice that we can all make. By approaching interactions with a sense of appreciation and openness, we have the power to create a more positive and uplifting environment for everyone. I am committed to continuing to practice gratitude and humility in my own life, and I encourage others to do the same. Together, we can make a positive impact on the world.

Embrace challenges to maintain a positive attitude with determination

Humility and Gratitude

Once upon a time, in a small town where I grew up among rolling hills, I was known for my talent and intelligence, but what set me apart from others was my unwavering humility. No matter the circumstances, I always found a way to embrace life with grace and gratitude.

One cloudy morning, I woke up to the news that I had been discriminated from my job. Instead of wallowing in self-pity, I saw this as an opportunity for growth. With humble determination, I began searching for new avenues to showcase my skills and contribute to society. I attended networking events, reached out to industry professionals, and took courses to enhance my knowledge.

During this time, I found my inner strength and write poetry and shared stories of how humility had shaped my own life. I emphasized that humility does not mean thinking less of oneself, but rather thinking of oneself less. I explained that by embracing humility, one can open doors to new perspectives and possibilities.

I was inspired by my writing and decided to volunteer at a local charity organization. Through selfless acts of service, I discovered a deeper sense of fulfillment and purpose. As I helped those less fortunate, I realized that humility allowed him to truly connect with others and understand their struggles.

Months passed, and my dedication and humility paid off. I received multiple job offers from companies impressed by my positive attitude and willingness to learn. However, instead of taking the most lucrative offer, I chose a position that aligned with my passion for helping others. With my humility intact, I knew I could make a real difference in people's lives.

As years went by, my reputation as a compassionate and humble individual spread far and wide. People sought my advice on various matters, knowing that my humility would guide me to offer unbiased and sage counsel. I became a mentor to many, teaching them the power of humility in embracing the circumstances of life.

Through ups and downs, I never forgot my humble beginnings. I remained grounded, always ready to lend a helping hand and listen attentively. My humility had become a guiding light, illuminating my path through life's challenges.

In conclusion, my story teaches us the profound impact humility can have on our lives. It reminds us to approach each day with gratitude, embrace difficult circumstances with grace, and find strength in our ability to connect with others. By cultivating humility, we not only achieve personal growth but also create a ripple effect of kindness and understanding that transforms our world for the better.

The journey is not easy, but it's a uphill battle

Poem

In a world of ego and pride,

Humility and gratitude reside.

They are virtues that shine so bright,

Guiding us through the darkest night.

Humility, a gentle and humble heart,

Acknowledging others' worth and art.

It's not about being small or weak,

But embracing the strength that's unique.

Gratitude, a grateful soul's embrace,

Finding joy in every little trace.

It's not about having everything in store,

But appreciating what we have and more.

Humility teaches us to be kind,

To treat others with an open mind.

It reminds us that we're all the same,

No one is above or below in this game.

Embrace challenges to maintain a positive attitude with determination

The journey is not easy, but it's a uphill battle

Gratitude reminds us to be thankful,

For the blessings, big and small, so delightful.

It fills our hearts with love and grace,

And brings a smile to our face.

Together, humility and gratitude,

Create a life of abundance and plenitude.

They remind us of our humanity,

And bring us closer to our divinity.

So let us practice these virtues each day,

In every word we speak and every step we sway.

For humility and gratitude, they hold the key,

To a life filled with love, joy, and harmony.

Embrace challenges to maintain a positive attitude with
determination

Overcoming Depression

Today, I find myself reflecting on a journey that has been both challenging and transformational – my battle with depression. It has been a constant companion, casting a shadow over my days and weighing heavily on my heart. But amidst the darkness, I have discovered a strength within me that I never knew existed.

Depression, like a heavy fog, has often clouded my mind and made even the simplest tasks seem insurmountable. It has whispered lies of worthlessness and hopelessness, making it difficult to see any light at the end of the tunnel. But I refuse to let it define me. I am determined to find a way out.

In my quest to overcome depression, I have learned that seeking help is not a sign of weakness but a courageous act of self-care. I reached out to a therapist who provided a safe space for me to express my deepest fears and emotions. Through therapy, I gained valuable insights into the root causes of my depression and developed coping mechanisms to navigate through the darkest moments.

One of the most significant steps I took in my journey was to build a support system. I confided in my loved ones, sharing my struggles and allowing them to offer their unwavering support. Their love and understanding became a lifeline, reminding me that I was not alone in this battle. Their presence has been a constant source of comfort and encouragement.

Embrace challenges to maintain a positive attitude with determination

The journey is not easy, but it's a uphill battle

Another crucial aspect of my recovery has been self-care. I have learned to prioritize my physical and mental well-being. Engaging in activities that bring me joy and peace, such as exercise, meditation, and creative outlets, has helped me regain a sense of control and purpose. Taking care of myself has become a non-negotiable part of my daily routine.

Additionally, I have found solace in practicing gratitude. Each day, I make a conscious effort to focus on the positive aspects of my life, no matter how small they may seem. Gratitude has shifted my perspective, allowing me to appreciate the beauty and blessings that surround me. It has reminded me that even in the midst of darkness, there is always a glimmer of light.

While the journey to overcome depression is far from linear, I have come to understand that setbacks are a natural part of the process. On days when the weight feels unbearable, I remind myself to be patient and gentle with myself. I celebrate the small victories and acknowledge that healing takes time.

Today, as I write this journal entry, I am filled with a renewed sense of hope and resilience. I have come a long way, and though the road ahead may still be challenging, I am armed with the tools and support to face whatever comes my way. I am no longer defined by my depression but by my strength and determination to overcome it.

I am grateful for this journey, as it has taught me the power of self-discovery, resilience, and the importance of

Embrace challenges to maintain a positive attitude with determination

The journey is not easy, but it's a uphill battle

reaching out for help. I am proud of the progress I have made, and I look forward to the future with a newfound sense of optimism.

Remember, if you are struggling with depression, you are not alone. Reach out, seek help, and believe in your own strength. There is light at the end of the tunnel, and you have the power to overcome.

Embrace challenges to maintain a positive attitude with determination

Being an Influence and Role Model

Nowadays, I find myself reflecting on the power we have to influence others and be a positive role model, regardless of our circumstances. It is a responsibility that I embrace wholeheartedly, as I believe that our actions and words can shape the lives of those around us.

Influence is not about having a position of authority or a large following. It is about the impact we have on the people we encounter, whether it be our family, friends, colleagues, or even strangers. It is a reminder that our words and actions hold weight and can inspire change.

To become an influence and role model, I have learned that authenticity is key. It is important to stay true to myself and live in alignment with my values. By being genuine and transparent, I create a foundation of trust and credibility. People are more likely to be influenced by someone they perceive as authentic and sincere.

Another aspect of being a determinant is leading by example. I strive to embody the qualities and values I wish to see in others. Whether it is kindness, resilience, or empathy, I understand that my actions speak louder than words. By consistently demonstrating these qualities, I inspire others to follow suit.

I also recognize the power of empathy and active listening. To truly influence others, I must first understand their perspectives and experiences. By listening attentively and empathizing with their challenges, I create a space for open dialogue and mutual understanding. This allows me to offer guidance and support in a meaningful way.

Influence is not about forcing my opinions onto others, but rather empowering them to think critically and make informed decisions. I encourage open-mindedness and respect diverse viewpoints. By fostering an environment of inclusive and acceptance, I create opportunities for growth and collaboration.

Regardless of the circumstances I may face, I believe that I can still be a determined person and role model. Adversity does not define me; it is how I respond to it that matters. In times of difficulty, I strive to maintain a positive mindset and find solutions rather than dwelling on the challenges. By demonstrating resilience and perseverance, I inspire others to do the same.

Lastly, I understand the importance of continuous personal growth and self-reflection. To be an effective influence, I must constantly learn and evolve. I seek out opportunities for self-improvement, whether through reading, attending workshops, or seeking guidance from mentors. By investing in my own growth, I am better equipped to inspire and guide others.

As I conclude, I am reminded of the immense privilege and responsibility that comes with being an influence and role model. I am committed to using my influence for the betterment of others and to uplift and

The journey is not easy, but it's a uphill battle

empower those around me. No matter the circumstances, I believe that each of us has the power to make a positive impact and be a guiding light in the lives of others.

Remember, you have the ability to influence and be a role model, regardless of your circumstances. Embrace your authenticity, lead by example, listen with empathy, and continuously grow. Together, we can create a ripple effect of positive change in the world.

Embrace challenges to maintain a positive attitude with determination

The journey is not easy, but it's a uphill battle

Poem

In a world that moves so fast,

I find solace in a passion that lasts.

For when I immerse myself in what I love,

I soar high on wings like a graceful dove.

Passion, a fire that burns within,

Igniting my soul, where possibilities begin.

It fuels my dreams, it lights my way,

Guiding me through each and every day.

In every endeavor, big or small,

Passion is the driving force that calls.

It breathes life into my every action,

Infusing purpose and satisfaction.

When I'm passionate, I give my all,

Breaking down barriers, standing tall.

Obstacles become mere stepping stones,

As I pursue my dreams with heart and bones.

Embrace challenges to maintain a positive attitude with
determination

The journey is not easy, but it's a uphill battle

Passion fuels creativity's flame,

Transforming the ordinary into something untamed.

With every stroke of brush or pen,

I create a world where magic begins.

In the pursuit of passion, I find my voice,

A melody that resonates, a choice.

It speaks of authenticity and truth,

Inspiring others to follow suit.

Passion is contagious, it spreads like wildfire,

Igniting the hearts of those who aspire.

It sparks curiosity, it fuels desire,

To explore, to learn, to reach higher.

So, I embrace my passions, big and small,

For they are the essence of my soul's call.

With every breath, I let them ignite,

A fire within that burns so bright.

Embrace challenges to maintain a positive attitude with determination

The journey is not easy, but it's a uphill battle

For in passion, I find purpose and meaning,

A life that's vibrant, constantly gleaming.

So, I encourage you, dear friend, to pursue,

Your passions, for they will guide you true.

Let your heart be the compass, your soul the guide,

And let passion be the fuel that propels you wide.

Embrace the joy, the thrill, the zest,

And watch as your life becomes truly blessed.

Embrace challenges to maintain a positive attitude with
determination

The journey is not easy, but it's a uphill battle

Overcoming Discouragement

Today was a challenging day, filled with moments of discouragement and self-doubt. However, I am determined to rise above these negative feelings and find the strength to overcome them. In this journal entry, I will explore different strategies and techniques that can help me overcome discouragement and regain my motivation.

Recognize and Accept Feelings: The first step in overcoming discouragement is acknowledging and accepting the emotions that come with it. It's okay to feel down or disappointed, but it's essential not to dwell on these feelings for too long. By recognizing them and giving them space, I can begin to work towards finding a solution.

Seek Support: It's important to remember that I don't have to face these challenges alone. Seeking support from loved ones, friends, or even professional counselors can provide a fresh perspective and valuable advice. Sharing my feelings with someone who understands can be incredibly empowering and uplifting.

Reframe Negative Thoughts: Our thoughts have a powerful impact on our emotions. When faced with discouragement, it's crucial to challenge negative thoughts and replace them with positive and realistic ones. Reminding myself of past successes and focusing on my strengths can help shift my mindset and regain confidence.

Embrace challenges to maintain a positive attitude with determination

The journey is not easy, but it's a uphill battle

Set Realistic Goals: Setting realistic and achievable goals can help break down overwhelming tasks into smaller, more manageable steps. By setting clear objectives and celebrating small victories along the way, I can maintain a sense of progress and motivation.

Embrace Failure as a Learning Opportunity:

Discouragement often stems from setbacks or perceived failures. However, it's important to remember that failure is an essential part of growth and learning. Instead of dwelling on mistakes, I will choose to view them as valuable lessons that can propel me forward.

Practice Self-Care: Taking care of myself physically, mentally, and emotionally is crucial in overcoming discouragement. Engaging in activities that bring me joy, such as exercise, hobbies, or spending time in nature, can help rejuvenate my spirit and provide a much-needed break from negative thoughts.

Stay Persistent and Resilient: Overcoming discouragement requires persistence and resilience. It's important to keep pushing forward, even when faced with obstacles or setbacks. Reminding myself of my long-term goals and the reasons why I started this journey in the first place can help me stay motivated and focused.

In conclusion, I am reminded that overcoming discouragement is a journey, not a destination. It requires patience, self-compassion, and a willingness to learn and grow. By implementing these strategies and techniques, I

Embrace challenges to maintain a positive attitude with determination

am confident that I can overcome any obstacles that come my way and continue to pursue my dreams with renewed vigor and determination.

I want to share some thoughts on a topic that often affects us all – discouragement. Life is full of challenges and setbacks, and it's natural to feel discouraged at times. However, it's crucial to find ways to overcome these feelings and keep moving forward. Here are a few strategies that have helped me in my journey:

Acknowledge your emotions:

It's important to acknowledge and validate your feelings of discouragement. Don't suppress them or pretend they don't exist. Recognize that it's okay to feel down sometimes, but also remind yourself that you have the power to change your mindset.

Reflect on past successes: Take a moment to reflect on your past accomplishments and successes. Remembering your achievements can help you regain confidence and remind yourself that you are capable of overcoming challenges.

Set realistic goals: Break down your larger goals into smaller, manageable tasks. This will help you experience progress along the way and give you a sense of accomplishment. Celebrate these small victories, as they will propel you forward.

Surround yourself with positive people: Surround yourself with positive people who uplift and encourage you.

Embrace challenges to maintain a positive attitude with determination

Their support can make a significant difference during difficult times. Additionally, seek out inspirational stories or quotes that resonate with you. They can serve as a reminder that others have faced similar struggles and triumphed.

Practice self-care: Take care of yourself both physically and mentally. Engage in activities that bring you joy and relaxation. Exercise regularly, eat well, get enough sleep, and dedicate time to hobbies or interests that rejuvenate your spirit. Taking care of yourself will not only boost your mood but also equip you with the energy needed to face challenges.

Seek support: Don't hesitate to reach out to friends, family, or a trusted mentor for support and guidance. Sometimes, talking about your feelings with someone who understands can provide valuable insights or simply provide comfort during tough times.

Learn from setbacks: View setbacks as opportunities for growth and learning. Analyze what went wrong, identify lessons you can take away from the experience, and use those lessons to improve and move forward. Remember, failure is not final as long as you learn from it.

Stay optimistic: Cultivate an optimistic mindset and believe in your ability to overcome adversity. Focus on the positive aspects of your life and practice gratitude. Remind yourself of the progress you have made and trust that you have the strength and resilience to overcome any obstacle.

Embrace challenges to maintain a positive attitude with determination

The journey is not easy, but it's a uphill battle

As I conclude this method, I'm reminded that everyone faces discouragement at some point in their lives. However, it is how we choose to respond to these challenges that make all the difference. By implementing these strategies and maintaining a positive outlook, we can overcome discouragement and continue to grow and thrive.

Remember, you are stronger than you think, and the power to overcome lies within you. Stay hopeful, and keep moving forward!

Embrace challenges to maintain a positive attitude with determination

The Power of Waiting for Miracles:

Life is a journey filled with uncertainties and challenges, but amidst it all, we often find ourselves waiting for miracles. We yearn for that one extraordinary event that will change our lives, bring us joy, and spur us to celebrate the wonders life has to offer. But why do we wait for miracles? And what significance do they hold in our lives?

Miracles have the power to reshape our perspectives, renew our hope, and remind us of the beauty that lies within the realm of possibilities. They allow us to witness the extraordinary amidst the ordinary and help us appreciate the simple joys that surround us daily.

While waiting for a miracle, we are often tempted to succumb to doubt, impatience, or negativity. It is during these times that we must remember the importance of faith and perseverance. Miracles seldom arrive on our doorstep unannounced; they require us to actively participate in their creation.

When we embark on the path of waiting for miracles, we learn valuable life lessons. We discover the strength and resilience that lie deep within us. We develop patience, endurance, and a newfound appreciation for the present moment. The process of waiting teaches us to have faith and trust in the universe, knowing that things will unfold in due course.

The journey is not easy, but it's a uphill battle

Furthermore, the act of waiting for miracles allows us to reflect on our goals, desires, and aspirations. It prompts us to evaluate our actions, align them with our intentions, and make necessary adjustments. Instead of passively waiting, we become active participants in shaping our own destinies.

Waiting for miracles also gives us an opportunity to celebrate our lives. It encourages us to find joy in the journey itself rather than solely focusing on the destination. Each day becomes a cause for celebration as we acknowledge the blessings we have, even before the miracle arrives.

In this fast-paced world, we often overlook the little miracles that happen all around us. The blooming of a flower, a heartfelt conversation, or a sunset painting the sky in hues of gold — these are the everyday miracles that remind us of life's extraordinary nature. When we cultivate an attitude of gratitude and remain open to the miracles that unfold daily, life becomes a continuous celebration.

So, as we wait for that grand miracle, let us not forget to celebrate the smaller miracles along the way. Let us embrace the challenges, cherish the lessons, and find solace in the belief that miracles are always within reach.

Remember, dear journal, life is meant to be celebrated — whether it is through waiting for the extraordinary or reveling in the ordinary. May our hearts be filled with gratitude, hope, and an unwavering belief in the power of miracles.

Embrace challenges to maintain a positive attitude with determination

The journey is not easy, but it's a uphill battle

With love and anticipation,

Embrace challenges to maintain a positive attitude with
determination

Waiting on miracles

The act of waiting for miracles can have a profound impact on our perspective on life and the challenges we face. It instills in us a sense of hope and optimism, reminding us that there is always a possibility for something extraordinary to occur. When we believe in the power of miracles and actively wait for them, we approach life's challenges with a renewed sense of faith and determination. We become more resilient as we are willing to persevere through difficult times, knowing that a miracle may be right around the corner. Additionally, the act of waiting for miracles encourages us to live in the present moment and appreciate the beauty and wonder in everyday life. It helps us cultivate gratitude and a deep appreciation for the small joys and blessings that surround us. Ultimately, waiting for miracles expands our perspective and reminds us that life is full of possibilities and opportunities for growth and transformation.

The act of waiting for miracles can shape our perspective on life and the challenges we encounter in several ways. Firstly, it reminds us to maintain hope and optimism even in difficult times. When we believe in the possibility of miracles, we are more likely to approach challenges with a positive mindset and look for solutions rather than dwelling on negativity.

Embrace challenges to maintain a positive attitude with determination

Secondly, waiting for miracles teaches us the importance of patience and perseverance. Miracles often take time to unfold, and the process of waiting can be an opportunity for personal growth and self-discovery. It encourages us to have faith and trust that things will work out in their own time, even if the outcome is not immediately apparent.

Additionally, waiting for miracles can help us develop a greater sense of gratitude and appreciation for the present moment. It encourages us to focus on the beauty and wonder that exists in everyday life rather than constantly striving for something in the future. This shift in perspective can lead to a deeper connection with ourselves and the world around us, enhancing our overall sense of fulfillment and happiness.

Lastly, waiting for miracles expands our perspective by reminding us that life is full of possibilities and opportunities for growth and transformation. It encourages us to keep an open mind and be receptive to unexpected blessings and synchronicity. By embracing the idea that miracles can happen at any moment, we become more receptive to new experiences and more willing to step outside of our comfort zones.

Overall, waiting for miracles can shape our perspective on life and the challenges we encounter by fostering hope, patience, gratitude, and an openness to new possibilities. It reminds us that life is a journey filled with

The journey is not easy, but it's a uphill battle

both struggles and blessings and that every moment has the potential for magic and transformation.

Maintaining hope and optimism in difficult times is important because it allows us to stay positive and motivated. It gives us the strength to keep moving forward, even when faced with challenges and setbacks. Hope and optimism help us believe that things will eventually get better and that we have the ability to overcome obstacles. They also provide a sense of comfort and resilience, helping us cope with stress and adversity. Overall, maintaining hope and optimism can improve our mental well-being and increase our chances of finding solutions and opportunities in difficult times.

Embrace challenges to maintain a positive attitude with determination

Poem

In this journey called life, we embark,

Through moments of joy and times so dark.

With every step we take, a story unfolds,

A tale of love, courage, and dreams untold.

Like a river flowing through the land,

Life meanders, guided by nature's hand.

It teaches us lessons, both gentle and tough,

And reminds us that we are made of resilient stuff.

We face challenges, hurdles in our way,

Yet find strength to overcome each day.

For in our hearts, a fire burns bright,

Igniting our spirits to reach new heights.

Life's canvas is painted with colors diverse,

Each moment a blessing, a gift to immerse.

From sunrise to sunset, the beauty we see,

The journey is not easy, but it's a uphill battle

We learn to cherish every opportunity.

Through laughter and tears, we find solace within,

Embracing the highs and lows, we begin.

To appreciate the beauty in simple things,

And the happiness that everyday life brings.

So let us treasure this life we share,

With compassion, kindness, and love to spare.

For in this grand tapestry we weave,

Our lives intertwine, and together, we believe.

Embrace challenges to maintain a positive attitude with
determination

How can we find the courage to pursue our dreams amidst life's uncertainties?

Finding the courage to pursue our dreams amidst life's uncertainties can be challenging, but there are a few things we can do to help ourselves. Firstly, it's important to remember that uncertainty is a natural part of life and often accompanies growth and change.

To find courage, it can be helpful to break down our dreams into smaller, achievable goals. By focusing on the steps we can take in the present moment, we can build momentum and overcome any fears or doubts. It's also essential to surround ourselves with supportive and positive people who believe in us and our dreams. Their encouragement and belief can provide us with the strength to keep going, even when things get tough.

Additionally, taking care of our physical and mental well-being is crucial. Engaging in self-care practices such as exercise, meditation, or hobbies helps to reduce stress and maintain a positive mindset. By prioritizing our health and well-being, we can better navigate the uncertainties that come our way.

Lastly, remember that setbacks and failures are often part of the journey. Instead of viewing them as roadblocks, see them as opportunities for growth and

The journey is not easy, but it's a uphill battle

learning. Embrace the unknown, stay resilient, and have faith in yourself and your abilities. With determination and perseverance, you can find the courage to pursue your dreams, no matter what uncertainties life may bring.

Embrace challenges to maintain a positive attitude with determination

What are some specific strategies for redirecting your energy toward things you can influence?

One strategy for redirecting your energy towards things you can influence is to focus on what you can control. This means identifying the aspects of a situation that you have power over and putting your energy into those areas. For example, if you're feeling frustrated about a work project, instead of focusing on the things you can't control (like your coworker's actions), focus on what you can control, such as your own work ethic and approach.

Another strategy is to practice acceptance and letting go. Recognize that there are things in life that are outside of your control, and instead of expending energy on them, learn to accept them and focus on what you can change. This can help you avoid unnecessary stress and frustration.

Additionally, setting realistic goals and breaking them down into smaller, actionable steps can help you direct your energy in a productive way. By focusing on specific tasks or actions that you can take, you can make progress towards your goals and feel more empowered.

Finally, surrounding yourself with supportive and positive people can also help redirect your energy. Engaging in conversations and activities that uplift and inspire you can

The journey is not easy, but it's a uphill battle

shift your mindset towards the things you can influence and motivate you to take action.

Remember, redirecting your energy toward things you can influence takes practice and patience. It's important to be kind to yourself and celebrate small victories along the way.

Embrace challenges to maintain a positive attitude with determination

The journey is not easy, but it's a uphill battle

Can you provide examples of specific situations where focusing on what you can control can lead to a more positive outcome?

Job search: Instead of worrying about whether you'll get the job offer, focus on preparing for interviews and improving your resume. This will increase your chances of getting hired.

Relationships: Rather than trying to change someone else's behavior, focus on improving your own communication skills and being more understanding. This can lead to better relationships and more positive interactions.

Health and fitness: Instead of fixating on the number on the scale, concentrate on making healthier choices like eating nutritious meals and exercising regularly. This can result in improved overall well-being.

Personal goals: Instead of dwelling on external circumstances that may be out of your control, concentrate on setting achievable goals and taking consistent steps towards them. This can lead to a sense of accomplishment and increased motivation.

Embrace challenges to maintain a positive attitude with determination

The journey is not easy, but it's a uphill battle

Remember, focusing on what you can control allows you to take ownership of your actions and outcomes, leading to a more positive and empowered mindset.

Embrace challenges to maintain a positive attitude with determination

The journey is not easy, but it's a uphill battle

Poem

In the depths of doubt and despair,

When motivation seems so rare,

Remember, my friend, you have the power,

To rise above and bloom like a flower.

Embrace the fire that burns within,

Let it ignite your dreams, let it begin,

With every step, with every stride,

You'll find the strength to reach the sky.

When obstacles appear on your way,

Let inspiration guide you, day by day,

Seek wisdom from those who gone before,

Their stories will ignite your core.

In moments of darkness, don't lose sight,

For inspiration can be found, even in the night,

Look to the stars, their brilliance so bright,

They remind you to keep reaching for new heights.

Embrace challenges to maintain a positive attitude with
determination

The journey is not easy, but it's a uphill battle

Surround yourself with positive souls,

Whose encouragement uplifts and consoles,

Together, you'll create a symphony of dreams,

A harmony that empowers and redeems.

Take care of yourself, both body and mind,

For without self-care, motivation is hard to find,

Nurture your soul with love and rest,

And watch as motivation becomes your quest.

Challenge the doubts that hold you back,

Replace them with beliefs that keep you on track,

Let failure be your stepping stone,

To learn, to grow, and to make your own.

So, my dear friend, stay motivated and inspired,

Let your dreams burn bright, never be tired,

Believe in yourself, and let your spirit soar,

For with determination, success is yours to explore.

Embrace challenges to maintain a positive attitude with
determination

My Passion for Helping Others

Reflecting on my deep-seated passion for helping others, it is a driving force in my life, and it brings me immense joy and fulfillment. In this journal entry, I will explore the reasons behind this passion and the impact it has on both myself and those I strive to assist.

The Joy of Making a Difference: There is an indescribable joy that comes from knowing that I have positively impacted someone's life. Whether it's through a small act of kindness or a more significant contribution, the feeling of making a difference is incredibly rewarding. It fuels my passion and motivates me to continue helping others.

Empathy and Compassion: My passion for helping others stems from a deep sense of empathy and compassion. I genuinely care about the well-being of others and find fulfillment in alleviating their struggles or bringing them comfort. It is through this empathy that I can connect with people on a deeper level and understand their needs.

Creating Meaningful Connections: Helping others allows me to forge meaningful connections with individuals from all walks of life. It enables me to step outside of my own experiences and learn from others' unique perspectives. These connections enrich my life and broaden my understanding of the world.

Personal Growth and Learning: When I help others, I am not only impacting their lives but also my own. It

The journey is not easy, but it's a uphill battle

provides me with opportunities for personal growth and self-discovery. Through helping others, I learn valuable lessons about resilience, empathy, and the power of human connection.

Being a Catalyst for Change: My passion for helping others also stems from a desire to be a catalyst for positive change in the world. I believe that even small acts of kindness can have a ripple effect, inspiring others to pay it forward and creating a chain reaction of goodness.

Fulfilling a Sense of Purpose: Helping others gives me a sense of purpose and meaning in life. It allows me to align my actions with my values and make a tangible impact on the lives of others. This sense of purpose drives me forward, even in the face of challenges or setbacks.

Spreading Positivity and Hope: In a world that can sometimes feel overwhelming and disheartening, my passion for helping others allows me to spread positivity and hope. By offering support, encouragement, and a helping hand, I strive to make the world a brighter and more compassionate place.

In conclusion, I am reminded of the immense privilege and responsibility that comes with my passion for helping others. It is a lifelong journey that requires continuous learning, growth, and self-reflection. However, the rewards are immeasurable, and I am grateful for the opportunity to make a positive impact on the lives of others.

Embrace challenges to maintain a positive attitude with determination

Poem

In the depths of heartbreak's dark embrace,

When love's light seems a distant trace,

A flicker of hope begins to ignite,

A chance to heal, to soar, to take flight.

For in the wake of shattered dreams,

New beginnings await, it seems,

A chance to mend the broken parts,

To find solace in tender, mending hearts.

It takes courage to open up again,

To trust, to love, to feel the pain,

But within each crack, a strength does grow,

A resilience that only heartbreak can bestow.

Give a chance to love's sweet refrain,

To dance upon the soul's terrain,

Allow the wounds to slowly fade,

Embrace challenges to maintain a positive attitude with determination

The journey is not easy, but it's a uphill battle

As new love's melody is gently played.

For in the realm of second tries,

True healing and growth often lie,

A chance to learn, to rise above,

And rediscover the power of love.

Though scars may linger, etched in time,

They tell a story of strength sublime,

So let the heartbreak be a guide,

To a love that's deeper, unswayed by tides.

Give a chance to the whispers of fate,

To rewrite the story, to recreate,

For sometimes, in the midst of the ache,

A chance emerges, a love to partake.

So take a breath, embrace the unknown,

For in vulnerability, seeds are sown,

Give a chance, and let love's light ignite,

A chance to heal, to love, to take flight.

Embrace challenges to maintain a positive attitude with determination

Nurturing Self-Care through Setting Boundaries

Today, I find myself reflecting on the importance of setting boundaries in my life. Boundaries are the invisible lines that define and protect my physical, emotional, and mental well-being. They serve as a means of self-care, allowing me to nurture myself and maintain healthy relationships with others. As I navigate this journey of personal growth, I am reminded of the power and necessity of establishing and maintaining boundaries.

Setting boundaries is an act of self-love and self-respect. It is recognizing and acknowledging my own needs and limitations, and honoring them without guilt or apology. By defining my own limits, I create a safe and healthy space where I can thrive and grow. It is not a selfish act, but rather a necessary step towards maintaining my own well-being and preserving my energy and sanity.

One of the key aspects of setting boundaries is understanding my own values and priorities. By clarifying what is truly important to me, I can establish boundaries that align with my core beliefs and goals. This clarity empowers me to make choices that honor my values and protect my time and energy from being consumed by activities or relationships that do not serve me in a positive way.

Another vital aspect of setting boundaries is effective communication. It is important to clearly and assertively communicate my boundaries to others, while also respecting their boundaries in return. Open and honest communication allows for mutual understanding and helps to build healthy and respectful relationships. It provides an opportunity for dialogue, negotiation, and compromise when necessary.

I recognize that setting boundaries may not always be easy. It can be uncomfortable, especially when it involves saying "no" or disappointing others. However, I remind myself that prioritizing my own well-being is essential. It is not my responsibility to constantly please others at the expense of my own happiness and peace of mind. By setting boundaries, I am taking ownership of my own needs and emotions and fostering a sense of empowerment and self-worth.

Boundaries also serve as a means of self-protection. They create a shield against toxic relationships, negative influences, and draining situations. Setting boundaries allows me to create a space where I feel safe, respected, and valued. It helps me to identify and address behaviors or

The journey is not easy, but it's a uphill battle

situations that are not in alignment with my well-being, and to make conscious choices that promote my growth and happiness.

As I conclude, I am reminded of the ongoing journey of setting and maintaining boundaries. It is a continuous practice that requires self-awareness, self-compassion, and self-assertion. It is a process of learning and growing, of discovering what nourishes my soul and what depletes it. I am committed to nurturing myself through the establishment of healthy boundaries, embracing the power and freedom that comes with honoring my own needs and desires.

Remember, dear journal, that setting boundaries is an act of self-care and self-respect. It is a means of protecting my well-being and creating a life that is aligned with my values and priorities. May I continue to embrace the journey of setting boundaries, cultivating healthy relationships, and nurturing my own growth and happiness?

Embrace challenges to maintain a positive attitude with determination

The journey is not easy, but it's a uphill battle

Poem

In the depths of my being, a flame burns bright,

A fire of self-respect, a guiding light.

For I am worthy, deserving of love and care,

A soul deserving of reverence beyond compare.

With each step I take, I honor my worth,

Embracing my essence, my inherent birth.

For self-respect is the foundation of my soul,

A pillar of strength, making me whole.

I stand tall, unyielding in my truth,

Embracing my flaws, my imperfections, uncouth.

For in accepting myself, both light and shade,

I find the beauty in the journey I've made.

I set boundaries, firm and clear,

Preserving my dignity, without fear.

For self-respect demands that I stand strong,

Embrace challenges to maintain a positive attitude with
determination

The journey is not easy, but it's a uphill battle

Protecting my spirit, where I belong.

I listen to the whispers of my heart,

Honoring my values, refusing to depart.

For self-respect calls me to be true,

To live authentically, in all that I pursue.

I choose relationships that lift me higher,

Where respect and love fuel the fire.

For I deserve connections that nourish my soul,

Where mutual respect and kindness take their toll.

I speak my truth, with confidence and grace,

Knowing my voice has a sacred place.

For self-respect empowers me to be heard,

To share my wisdom, my truth, my word.

I care for myself, body, mind, and soul,

Nurturing my being, making me whole.

For self-respect demands self-care,

A tender embrace, showing myself I'm aware.

Embrace challenges to maintain a positive attitude with
determination

The journey is not easy, but it's a uphill battle

In the mirror, I see a reflection divine,

A soul worthy of love, a heart that shines.

For self-respect is the anthem I sing,

A melody of worth, a celebration of being.

So let us honor ourselves, with utmost regard,

Embracing self-respect as our guiding star.

For within our being, a treasure lies,

A deep self-respect that never dies.

Embrace challenges to maintain a positive attitude with
determination

The Importance of Genuine Concern for Diversity, Equality, and Inclusion

January 2024, I find myself reflecting on the significance of genuine concern for diversity, equality, and inclusion. It is essential to acknowledge that the impact of defamation of character can be detrimental to an individual's mental health and physical well-being. As I explore this topic, I am reminded of the importance of fostering a truly inclusive and empathetic society.

In our journey towards creating a more equitable world, it is crucial to prioritize the well-being of every individual. Genuine concern for diversity, equality, and inclusion goes beyond mere pretense. It requires an understanding of the profound impact that defamation of character can have on someone's life.

Defamation of character can inflict emotional distress, leading to anxiety, depression, and other mental health challenges. It can erode an individual's sense of self-worth, leaving them feeling isolated and vulnerable. The physical manifestations of such distress can manifest in various ways, including sleep disturbances, changes in appetite, and even physical illnesses. The consequences are far-reaching and can have a lasting impact on an individual's overall well-being.

To truly address the issue of defamation and its impact, it is crucial to foster a culture of empathy, understanding, and accountability. This begins with recognizing the power of our words and actions. Each of us has a responsibility to treat others with respect, compassion, and fairness. It is through genuine concern for diversity, equality, and inclusion that we can create an environment that promotes understanding and acceptance.

In our pursuit of justice and equality, we must also be vigilant in addressing instances of defamation and its consequences. This requires not only supporting those who have experienced harm but also actively working to prevent and educate others about the impact of defamation. By raising awareness and promoting empathy, we can build a society that values and respects the dignity and well-being of every individual.

In conclusion, I am reminded of the importance of genuine concern for diversity, equality, and inclusion. It is not enough to merely pretend to care; we must actively work towards creating a world where defamation of character has no place, and where the well-being of all individuals is prioritized. Let us strive to be advocates for those who have been harmed, fostering understanding, empathy, and inclusion in all aspects of our lives.

Remember that genuine concern for diversity, equality, and inclusion requires us to stand against the harm

The journey is not easy, but it's a uphill battle

caused by defamation. May we continue to learn, grow, and work towards a world where every individual's mental health and physical well-being are protected and nurtured.

Embrace challenges to maintain a positive attitude with determination

Heaven and hell are both states of mind. Within each individual, there exists the potential for experiencing both heavenly and hellish states based on their thoughts, emotions, and perceptions.

In the realm of the mind, heaven represents a state of peace, joy, contentment, and fulfillment. It is a mindset characterized by affirmative, gratitude, and acceptance. When one's thoughts are rooted in love, compassion, and kindness, they create a heavenly experience within themselves and in their interactions with others.

On the other hand, hell represents a state of suffering, negativity, and despair. It is a mindset fueled by fear, anger, resentment, and other negative emotions. When one's thoughts are consumed by self-doubt, jealousy, or hatred, they create a hellish experience within themselves and project it onto the world around them.

Ultimately, heaven and hell are not physical places but rather subjective experiences that can be shaped by our thoughts, beliefs, and actions. Each individual has the power to choose their state of mind and cultivate a more heavenly existence.

By practicing mindfulness, cultivating positive thoughts, and engaging in self-reflection, one can gradually shift their mindset from a hellish state to a more heavenly one. It requires effort, patience, and self-awareness to overcome negative patterns and cultivate a more positive and peaceful state of mind.

Remember, heaven and hell exist within us, and we have the ability to shape our own experiences. By nurturing positive thoughts, cultivating love and compassion, and seeking support when needed, one can strive towards a more heavenly mindset and find inner peace and fulfillment.

The journey is not easy, but it's a uphill battle

How can individuals cultivate a mindset rooted in love, compassion, and kindness to experience heavenly states of mind?

There are several ways individuals can cultivate a mindset rooted in love, compassion, and kindness. Here are a few suggestions:

Practice self-reflection: Take time to reflect on your thoughts, actions, and emotions. Be aware of any negative or unkind patterns and actively work on replacing them with more positive and compassionate ones.

Cultivate gratitude: Regularly express gratitude for the people, experiences, and things in your life. This can help shift your focus towards positive aspects and generate feelings of love and kindness.

Show acts of kindness: Engage in small acts of kindness, both towards yourself and others. This could be as simple as offering a kind word, helping someone in need, or practicing self-care regularly.

Embrace challenges to maintain a positive attitude with determination

The journey is not easy, but it's a uphill battle

Develop empathy: Try to understand others' perspectives and experiences. Put yourself in their shoes and practice empathetic listening. This can help foster compassion and understanding towards others.

Surround yourself with positive influences: Seek out positive role models, books, music, or communities that inspire and encourage love, compassion, and kindness. Surrounding yourself with like-minded individuals can make it easier to maintain a mindset rooted in these qualities.

Practice mindfulness and meditation: Incorporate regular mindfulness and meditation practices into your daily routine. This can help bring awareness to your thoughts and emotions, as well as promote a sense of calmness and inner peace.

Remember, cultivating a mindset rooted in love, compassion, and kindness is an ongoing process. It requires patience, self-awareness, and consistent effort. But with time and dedication, you can experience heavenly states of mind and find greater joy and fulfillment in life.

Embrace challenges to maintain a positive attitude with determination

In what ways can regularly expressing gratitude contribute to cultivating a mindset of love, compassion, and kindness?

Expressing gratitude regularly can contribute to cultivating a regularly expressing gratitude can contribute mindset of love to cultivating a mindset of love, compassion, and kindness in several ways.

Firstly, when we express gratitude, we acknowledge the positive aspects, compassion, and kindness in several ways.

Firstly, expressing gratitude helps shift our lives and direct our focus from what is lacking in our lives to focus towards the things we appreciate. This shifts what we already have. This shift in perspective allows us to shift our perspective from a mindset of lack or negativity to one of abundance and quality. This appreciates the abundance that surrounds us, fostering feelings of contentment and satisfaction. When we are grateful for change in perspective can help us develop a more positive and compassionate outlook towards ourselves and others.

Secondly, expressing gratitude for the people, opportunities, and blessings in our lives, we develop a sense of love and appreciation for fosters a sense of connection and empathy. When we express gratitude towards others, we do those things.

Thirdly, expressing gratitude promotes empathy and compassion towards others. When we recognize and acknowledge their kindness, support, and efforts. This recognition not only strengthens the positive impact others have on our lives, we become more aware of their needs and struggles. This awareness of our relationships also deepens our understanding and empathy towards others. It reminds us that we are all interconnected and encourages acts that can inspire us to act with kindness and compassion towards them, creating a ripple effect of love and understanding.

Lastly, expressing gratitude for kindness and compassion towards others. Also, expressing gratitude helps us cultivate mindfulness and presence. Focusing on this helps cultivate a positive mindset. When we regularly acknowledge what we are grateful for in the present moment, we become more aware of the beauty and appreciate the good things in our lives, and our thoughts tend to gravitate towards positive determination and optimism. This positive mindset can influence our interactions with the goodness around us. This mindfulness allows us to fully appreciate the present moment and the people in our lives, fostering a greater sense of others and making us more open-warmhearted, kind, and loving in our relationships.

Overall, expressing gratitude for love, compassion, and kindness:

Overall, regularly expressing gratitude helps us develop a regularly serves as a powerful tool for cultivating a mindset of love, compassion, and kindness. It helps us appreciate the present moment, develop a positive mindset, deepen our connections with others, cultivate a greater sense of love, develop empathy towards others, and maintain a positive outlook on life, compassion, and kindness in our lives.

What are some examples of how expressing gratitude can help shift our focus from what is lacking in our lives?

Expressing gratitude can help shift our focus from what is in our lives by helping us to acknowledge and appreciate the positive aspects of our current situation. Here are some examples:

Increased mindfulness: When we actively express gratitude, it brings our attention to the present moment and helps us become more aware of the good things that surround us. This helps shift our focus away from what may be lacking and instead directs it toward the abundance we already have.

Positive mindset: Expressing gratitude encourages a positive outlook on life. By acknowledging and appreciating the blessings and opportunities we have, we naturally adopt a more optimistic attitude. This shift in mindset allows us to see possibilities and solutions rather than dwelling on what we don't have.

Deepened connections: Gratitude has the power to strengthen relationships and cultivate deeper connections with others. When we express gratitude towards someone, it not only makes them feel valued and appreciated, but it also fosters mutual trust and understanding. This shift in focus from what is lacking to acknowledging the presence of positive relationships enhances our overall well-being.

Enhanced empathy: Gratitude helps us develop empathy towards others by encouraging us to recognize and appreciate the kindness and support we receive from them. By shifting our focus from what is lacking to what we have, we become more sensitive to the needs and feelings of others, fostering a sense of compassion and empathy.

Improved overall well-being: The act of expressing gratitude has been linked to improved physical and mental health. When we focus on what we are grateful for, we experience a boost in positive emotions, reduced stress levels, increased resilience, and overall well-being. This shift in focus allows us to live more fulfilling and satisfying lives.

Embrace challenges to maintain a positive attitude with determination

The journey is not easy, but it's a uphill battle

By regularly practicing gratitude and consciously shifting our focus from what is lacking to what we are grateful for, we can cultivate a mindset of love, compassion, and kindness, ultimately transforming our lives for the better.

Embrace challenges to maintain a positive attitude with determination

How can acknowledging and appreciating the positive aspects of our situation enhance our overall well-being and happiness?

Acknowledging and appreciating the positive aspects of our situation can enhance our overall well-being and happiness in several ways.

Firstly, it helps to shift our perspective from a negative mindset to a positive one. When we consciously focus on what we are grateful for, we train our minds to see the good in every situation. This not only improves our mental well-being but also helps us to develop a more optimistic outlook on life.

Secondly, expressing gratitude can increase feelings of joy, contentment, and satisfaction. By acknowledging and appreciating the positive aspects of situation, we become more of the blessings and abundance our lives. This awareness can bring a sense fulfillment and happiness.

Furthermore, cultivating gratitude fosters a deeper connection with ourselves and. When we express gratitude towards others, we strengthen our relationships and build a sense community. This social support can greatly contribute to our overall well-being and happiness.

Additionally, practicing gratitude can help us cope with challenges and adversity. By focusing on what we are grateful for, we gain a sense of resilience and perspective, enabling us to navigate difficulties with more grace and ease.

In essence, when we acknowledge and appreciate the positive aspects of our situation, we invite more joy, satisfaction, and connection into our lives. By cultivating a mindset of gratitude, we can enhance our overall well-being and increase our levels of happiness.

Can developing a more optimistic outlook on life through acknowledging the positive aspects of our situation have long-term effects on our mental well-being?

Yes, developing a more optimistic outlook on life and acknowledging the positive aspects of our situation can have long-term effects on our mental well-being. Research has shown that practicing gratitude and focusing on the positive can lead to decreased levels of stress, anxiety, and depression. It can also improve our overall resilience, allowing us to better cope with challenges and bounce back from setbacks. In addition, adopting an optimistic mindset can enhance our relationships as we become more open and receptive to others, leading to increased social support and connectedness. So, by regularly practicing gratitude and

The journey is not easy, but it's a uphill battle

choosing to see the good in our lives, we can significantly contribute to our long-term mental well-being.

Embrace challenges to maintain a positive attitude with determination

Transforming Your Life: Changing Your Conditions through Self-Image

In our journey to personal growth and happiness, it is crucial to understand the power of self-image. How we perceive ourselves directly influences our actions, choices, and, ultimately, our life's conditions. By consciously changing our self-image, we can alter our entire reality, unlocking new opportunities and fulfilling our potential. This journal aims to guide you through the process of transforming your conditions by transforming your self-image.

Reflecting on Self-perception

Begin by introspecting and understanding your current self-image. Reflect on how you see yourself in different aspects of life – personally, professionally, and emotionally. Identify any negative or limiting beliefs that might be influencing your conditions.

Challenging Limiting Beliefs

Take a closer look at the negative beliefs you've identified. Are they rooted in objectively true facts or mere perceptions? Dissect these beliefs and challenge their validity. Replace them with positive affirmations based on your strengths, achievements, and potential.

Visualization and Affirmations

Visualize your ideal self and the conditions you wish to attain. Create a mental picture of yourself accomplishing your goals, living a fulfilling life, and embodying the characteristics you aspire to possess. Reinforce these visualizations with daily affirmations that align with your desired self-image.

Setting Meaningful Goals

Now that you have a clear vision of your ideal self, set meaningful goals that reflect this newly-formed self-image. Break down your goals into actionable steps and create a strategic plan to achieve them. Start taking small steps towards these goals consistently.

Embracing Self-Care

Prioritize self-care as an integral part of changing your self-image and conditions. Nurture your physical, mental, and emotional well-being through activities such as exercise, healthy eating, meditation, and engaging in hobbies that bring you joy. Taking care of yourself boosts self-confidence and reinforces a positive self-image.

Surrounding Yourself with Supportive Individuals

Evaluate your social circle and identify individuals who uplift and inspire you. Surround yourself with positive, supportive people who believe in your potential and

The journey is not easy, but it's a uphill battle

encourage your personal growth. Engage in open and meaningful conversations that foster a growth-oriented mindset.

Celebrating Progress and Gratitude

Acknowledge and celebrate the progress you've made throughout this journey. Gratitude plays a vital role in transforming your self-image as it helps you focus on what is going well in your life. Each day, write down at least three things you are grateful for and reflect on how they contribute to your overall well-being.

Conclusion:

Changing your conditions begins with changing your self-image. By actively working on reshaping how you perceive yourself and embracing a positive mindset, you can create a ripple effect that positively impacts your life's circumstances. Remember, growth and transformation take time and commitment, but with consistency and dedication, you can achieve the life you desire. Embrace this journal as a starting point in cultivating a powerful and empowering self-image.

Embrace challenges to maintain a positive attitude with determination

Body language is a powerful tool that can communicate a lot about us without the need for words. Here's a journal entry on how your body language can introduce you even without opening your mouth:

Speaking Volumes Without Words: The Power of Body Language

Body language is the unsung hero of communication, often overlooked but incredibly influential in how we are perceived by others. Today, I delved into the fascinating world of nonverbal cues and discovered just how much they can reveal about our personalities, confidence levels, and even our intentions.

It all starts with posture. Standing tall with an upright spine exudes confidence and shows that I am ready to take on any challenge that comes my way. Keeping my shoulders relaxed, but not slouched, sends a message of approach ability and puts others at ease in my presence. By maintaining eye contact, I establish a connection and show that I am fully engaged in the conversation.

I also explored the power of gestures. A firm handshake, for instance, can convey trustworthiness and professionalism right from the start. Open hand movements while speaking express openness and honesty, while crossed arms may unintentionally signal defensiveness or closed-mindedness. Mirroring the gestures of the person I am speaking with can create rapport and foster a sense of connection.

I then turned my attention to facial expressions. A warm smile can instantly make me more approachable and friendly. Smiling not only conveys happiness but also demonstrates that I genuinely enjoy interacting with others. Expressing genuine interest through attentive nods and raised eyebrows further reinforces this positive image.

Lastly, I explored the impact of personal space and proximity. Being aware of the appropriate distance to stand when speaking to someone helps establish boundaries and respect their personal comfort. Leaning slightly forward demonstrates interest and engagement, while leaning back may come across as disinterest or detachment.

Overall, I realized that my body language speaks volumes about me, often louder than any words I could utter. By consciously aligning my nonverbal cues with my intentions, I can introduce myself effectively and leave a lasting impression without ever opening my mouth. This newfound awareness has inspired me to refine my body

The journey is not easy, but it's a uphill battle

language skills further and continue on this journey of self-improvement.

Embrace challenges to maintain a positive attitude with determination

The journey is not easy, but it's a uphill battle

A poem about life struggles:

In the depths of life's relentless tide,

Where struggles dwell, and dreams collide,

We find ourselves in the midst of strife,

Battling through the storms of life.

With every step, a mountain to climb,

Challenges test the strength of our spine,

But within the struggle, we find our might,

A flame within, burning bright.

Life's struggles shape us, make us grow,

Teaching lessons we need to know,

Through hardships faced, we find our way,

Gaining wisdom with each passing day.

In the darkest nights, when hope seems lost,

We muster courage, no matter the cost,

For within the struggle lies our strength,

Embrace challenges to maintain a positive attitude with
determination

The journey is not easy, but it's a uphill battle

To rise above, go to any length.

Life's struggles may bend us, make us sway,

But they never define us, come what may,

For in the face of adversity's test,

We discover our resilience, our very best.

So let us embrace life's struggles with grace,

Knowing they lead us to a better place,

For it is through the battles we endure,

That our spirits rise, strong and pure.

Remember that life's struggles can be challenging, but they also provide opportunities for growth and resilience. Keep pushing forward, and never lose sight of your inner strength.

Embrace challenges to maintain a positive attitude with determination

The journey is not easy, but it's a uphill battle

Spoken words about motivation:

In the depths of doubt and fear,

When the path ahead is unclear,

Listen closely to the voice within,

For motivation is ready to begin.

Motivation, a flame deep inside,

Igniting dreams we cannot hide,

It whispers, "You have what it takes,

To conquer mountains and cross lakes."

When obstacles block your way,

And doubts cloud the light of day,

Motivation becomes your guiding star,

Leading you to who you truly are.

It says, "Rise up, embrace the fight,

With determination shining bright,

For every setback is just a chance,

Embrace challenges to maintain a positive attitude with
determination

The journey is not easy, but it's a uphill battle

To learn, to grow, to advance."

Motivation is the fuel you need,

To plant the seeds of success and heed,

The call to greatness, to soar high,

To reach for the limitless sky.

So let motivation be your guide,

In every step you take with pride,

Believe in yourself, trust your worth,

And let motivation propel you forth.

Remember, motivation is a powerful force that can drive you towards your goals and dreams. Embrace it, nurture it, and let it fuel your journey to success.

Embrace challenges to maintain a positive attitude with determination

The journey is not easy, but it's a uphill battle

Remaining Positive Through Difficult Circumstances

In the midst of storms and shadows deep,

I hold onto a promise I will keep.

A better day will come, I firmly believe,

No matter what challenges today may weave.

Though the road may be rough and steep,

I know that my faith I must keep.

For in the darkest hour, a glimmer of light,

Guides me through the struggles, shining so bright.

Today may bring trials, obstacles in my way,

But I choose to embrace them, come what may.

For each outcome, whether victory or defeat,

Holds lessons for me to learn and grow complete.

In every stumble, I find strength anew,

Embrace challenges to maintain a positive attitude with determination

The journey is not easy, but it's a uphill battle

Resilience and wisdom begin to accrue.

For it is through adversity that I find,

The power within me, unyielding and kind.

I embrace my outcome, whatever it may be,

For it shapes the person I am meant to see.

Each experience, a stepping stone on my path,

Leading me closer to my dreams, my aftermath.

I learn from the struggles, the mistakes I make,

They mold me, refine me, and help me awake.

To the possibilities that lie ahead,

A better version of myself, no longer misled.

So, I face today with courage and grace,

Knowing that a better day will embrace.

I embrace the challenges, the highs and lows,

For they shape my story, how it unfolds.

No matter what I face, I choose to believe,

Embrace challenges to maintain a positive attitude with
determination

The journey is not easy, but it's a uphill battle

That a better day will come, I will achieve.

With each lesson learned, I grow and evolve,

Embracing the journey, with problems I'll solve.

So, let us embrace our outcomes each day,

And learn from them in our unique way.

For a better day will come, this I know,

And with open hearts, we'll continue to grow.

Embrace challenges to maintain a positive attitude with determination

BACK COVER OF THE BOOK

The journey is not easy, but it's an uphill battle. Every step forward feels like a triumph, a small victory amidst the challenges that lie ahead. The path is filled with obstacles, testing both your physical and mental strength. But remember, it is in these moments of struggle that true growth occurs.

With each uphill battle, you gain resilience and determination. You learn to push through the fatigue, the doubt, and the fear. It is through these uphill battles that you discover your true potential and realize what you are truly capable of achieving.

Yes, the road may be long and arduous, but it is in this journey that you learn to appreciate the beauty of the climb. The view from the top becomes even more breathtaking when you have conquered the uphill battles along the way.

The journey is not easy, but it's in these challenges that you discover your strength, your courage, and your unwavering spirit. It is through the uphill battles that you transform into a better version of yourself, ready to take on whatever lies ahead.

So, embrace the difficulty, the sweat, and the tears. Embrace the uphill battle, for it is through this struggle that you find your true self. Keep moving forward, one step at a time, knowing that every uphill.

Embrace challenges to maintain a positive attitude with determination

The journey is not easy, but it's a uphill battle

Today, I find myself reflecting on journey that lies ahead It's not easy, that much is. There will be, obstacles, and moments of doubt the way. But I remind myself that every step forward, no matter how small, is progress.

I continue on this battle, I am of the strength within me I am capable of adversity, pushing past my comfort zone and reaching new heights. It may be tough at times, but I know that the rewards are worth it.

I am committed to facing each challenge head-on with courage and determination. I will not let fear or self-doubt hold me back. Instead, I will use them as fuel to propel me forward.

The journey may be daunting, but I embrace it wholeheartedly. I am ready to grow, learn, and evolve into the best version of myself. And with each step I take, I am one step closer to realizing my full potential.

Onward and upward,

Once upon a time, I struggled with rebuilding my strength. I had been facing difficult challenges and overwhelming emotions that led me to depression as a way of coping. One day, I realized that she needed to make a change and break free from this harmful behavior.

I decided to seek help and speak to a therapist who guided me toward healthier coping mechanisms. Through therapy, I learned how to identify my triggers, challenge

Embrace challenges to maintain a positive attitude with determination

negative thoughts, and practice self-compassion. I also surrounded herself with supportive friends and family who encouraged her on her journey to healing.

As I continued to work on myself and prioritize my mental health, I began to find new ways to cope with stress and emotions. I discovered the power of mindfulness, exercise, and creative outlets like painting and writing. Gradually, I stopped thinking negatively and started to embrace self-love and acceptance.

With time and effort, I was able to overcome my struggles and learn how to prioritize my well-being. I realized that I was worthy of love and happiness and that I had the strength to overcome any challenge that came my way. I hope my book serves as a reminder that with support, self-care, and resilience, it is possible to stop thinking negatively and create a life filled with joy and fulfillment.

The journey is not easy, but it's a uphill battle

Poem

In the midst of chaos, find solace within,

A refuge of peace, where calmness begins.

When life's storms rage and turmoil ensues,

Embrace the power within, and find your muse.

Breathe deeply, my dear, let the air fill your lungs,

Inhale the serenity; let it flow through your tongues.

Exhale the worries, the stress, and the strife,

Release the chaos, and embrace a new life.

Find comfort in nature, in its gentle embrace,

Feel the Earth's rhythm, its steady pace.

Listen to the whispers of the wind in the trees,

Let their soothing melody put your mind at ease.

Seek solace in silence, in moments of still,

Let your thoughts settle; let your heart be fulfilled.

For within the quiet, clarity will arise,

And chaos will dissolve, unveiling the skies.

Embrace challenges to maintain a positive attitude with determination

The journey is not easy, but it's a uphill battle

Write your emotions, let them spill on the page,

In the ink's embrace, find solace and engage.

Pour out your heart, release the inner storm,

And watch as calmness and peace begin to transform.

Find refuge in music, let its melodies heal,

Let the harmonies guide you; let them reveal

A symphony of tranquility, soothing your soul,

In the chaos, find rhythm, and let it console.

Embrace self-compassion, be gentle and kind,

For in chaos, your worth, you may find.

Treat yourself with love, as you would a friend,

Comfort your spirit, and let the chaos transcend.

In chaos, find comfort, for it is within,

A sanctuary of peace, where new beginnings begin.

Embrace the chaos, let it be your guide,

And find solace in yourself, where peace will reside.

Embrace challenges to maintain a positive attitude with
determination

Rising Above Adversity: My Journey as a Newly Promoted Sergeant

Introduction:

Life is a journey filled with ups and downs, and sometimes, we encounter challenges in unexpected places, such as the workplace. In this journal, I will recount my experience of being promoted to the position of sergeant in just 11 months and the difficulties I faced in navigating the changes and the treatment I received. Despite the challenges, I will share the strategies I employed to rise above the adversity and maintain my professionalism and self-worth.

The Excitement of Promotion

In the beginning, the news of my promotion to the rank of sergeant filled me with excitement and a sense of accomplishment. I was eager to take on new responsibilities and lead my team to success. I envisioned a supportive work environment where my efforts would be recognized and appreciated.

Unexpected Treatment

Unfortunately, my expectations were not met. Instead of receiving support and encouragement, I found myself facing hostility and unfair treatment from some of my colleagues. They questioned my abilities and belittled my achievements, undermining my confidence and creating a toxic work environment.

Navigating Adversity

In the face of adversity, I made a conscious decision to rise above the negativity and maintain my professionalism. I sought guidance from mentors and sought support from trusted colleagues who believed in my capabilities. Together, we developed strategies to address the challenges head-on and find constructive solutions.

Building Resilience

To build resilience, I focused on self-care and personal growth. I engaged in activities that brought me joy outside of work, such as hobbies and spending time with loved ones. I also sought opportunities for professional development to enhance my skills and knowledge, thus boosting my confidence in my abilities as a sergeant.

Leading by Example

As a sergeant, I understood the importance of leading by example. I remained committed to treating others with respect and fairness, regardless of how I was being treated. I fostered an inclusive and supportive environment within my team, providing a safe space for open communication and collaboration.

Seeking Resolution

Embrace challenges to maintain a positive attitude with determination

The journey is not easy, but it's a uphill battle

In my journey, I learned the importance of addressing issues directly and seeking resolution. I approached my superiors and HR department to express my concerns and provide evidence of the mistreatment I experienced. By advocating for myself, I hoped to bring about positive change not only for myself but for others who may face similar challenges.

Embracing Growth

Throughout this experience, I embraced personal growth and self-reflection. I recognized that adversity can be an opportunity for growth and self-improvement. I learned to use the challenges I faced as motivation to become a better leader and to cultivate a positive work environment for myself and my team.

Conclusion:

Although my journey as a newly promoted sergeant was marred by mistreatment and adversity, I remained resilient and determined to rise above the negativity. Through seeking support, maintaining professionalism, and advocating for change, I was able to navigate the challenges and create a positive work environment for myself and my team. I am proud of the growth I have achieved and the lessons I have learned along the way. This experience has strengthened my resolve to lead with compassion, fairness, and integrity, no matter the circumstances.

Embrace challenges to maintain a positive attitude with determination

Embracing Healing: My Journey Through Depression After Resignation

Life is filled with unexpected challenges, and sometimes, we find ourselves facing adversity in the workplace. In this journal, I will share my personal journey of dealing with depression after resigning from a job due to experiencing retaliation, defamation of character, and favoritism. It is my hope that my story will provide solace and inspiration to others who may have faced similar experiences.

The Breaking Point

In the beginning, I was enthusiastic about my job and eager to contribute to the success of the organization. However, as time passed, I began to experience retaliation from colleagues, who seemed threatened by my skills and dedication. The situation escalated when I became the target of defamation and character assassination. The injustice and favoritism I witnessed within the workplace became unbearable, leading me to make the difficult decision to resign.

The Weight of Emotional Turmoil

After my resignation, I found myself drowning in a sea of emotional turmoil. Depression engulfed me, and I struggled to find purpose and meaning in the aftermath of such a traumatic experience. I felt a deep sense of betrayal, confusion, and loss, which compounded my feelings of sadness and hopelessness.

Seeking Support

Recognizing the importance of seeking support, I reached out to trusted friends, family members, and mental health professionals. Their unwavering support and guidance provided me with a glimmer of hope during my darkest moments. They listened without judgment, offering a safe space for me to express my emotions and fears.

Embracing Self-Care

In my journey towards healing, I learned the significance of self-care. I prioritized activities that nourished my mind, body, and soul. Engaging in regular exercise, practicing mindfulness and meditation, and indulging in hobbies that brought me joy became essential pillars of my self-care routine. These activities provided moments of respite from the weight of depression.

Rediscovering Self-Worth

One of the greatest hurdles I faced during my battle with depression was reclaiming my self-worth. I reminded myself that the actions and opinions of others do not define my value as a person. Through self-reflection and therapy, I gradually rebuilt my self-esteem and began to recognize my strengths and capabilities once again.

Finding Purpose and Meaning

As I navigated my way through depression, I sought to find purpose and meaning in my life. I explored new interests, pursued personal goals, and engaged in volunteer work that aligned with my values. These experiences not only provided a sense of fulfillment but also reminded me of the positive impact I could make in the world.

Embracing Resilience

Throughout my journey, I discovered the power of resilience. I learned to view my experiences as opportunities for growth and personal development. I channeled my pain into advocacy, speaking out against workplace injustice and supporting others who have faced similar challenges. Through resilience, I found the strength and courage to create positive change.

Conclusion

My journey through depression after resigning due to retaliation, defamation of character, and favoritism has been a long and arduous one. However, it has also been a journey of self-discovery, healing, and empowerment. I have emerged from the depths of depression with a newfound sense of resilience and purpose. Although the scars of my experience may remain, they serve as a

The journey is not easy, but it's a uphill battle

reminder of my strength and resilience. I hope that my story inspires others to seek support, embrace self-care, and find their own path toward healing and happiness. Remember, you are not alone, and there is always hope for a brighter future.

Embrace challenges to maintain a positive attitude with determination

Poem

In the depths of despair, where shadows reside,

A tale of resilience, in darkness we confide.

A journey through pain, a battle within,

Depression's cruel grip, where hope feels thin.

Once upon a time, in a world so unjust,

I faced retaliation; my dreams turned to dust.

Defamation of character, a stain on my name,

And favoritism's poison, adding fuel to the flame.

Resigned from a job with a heavy heart,

Betrayed and broken, torn apart.

Depression's grip tightened, a suffocating hold,

In the depths of my despair, my story unfolds.

But from the ashes of darkness, a phoenix shall rise,

A spirit unyielding, with strength in its eyes.

I faced the abyss with courage so rare,

Embracing the battle, refusing to despair.

Embrace challenges to maintain a positive attitude with determination

The journey is not easy, but it's a uphill battle

In the depths of my sorrow, I sought out a light,

A glimmer of hope shone through the night.

Support and understanding from loved ones so true,

They held me up when I didn't know what to do.

I nurtured my soul with self-care and grace,

Embracing the healing at my own pace.

Meditation and mindfulness soothing my mind,

Exercise and hobbies, a sanctuary I find.

Through therapy's guidance, I confronted my pain,

Unraveled the layers, healing again.

Rediscovered my worth amidst the turmoil and strife,

For the actions of others don't define my life.

In the midst of the darkness, purpose I found,

To speak out against injustice, to make a resounding sound.

To lend a voice to those silenced and oppressed,

A beacon of hope for the ones distressed.

Embrace challenges to maintain a positive attitude with
determination

The journey is not easy, but it's a uphill battle

With resilience as my armor, I stood tall and strong,

Turning my battles into a triumphant song.

For in the depths of despair, seeds of strength do grow,

A testament to the human spirit's glow.

So, if you find yourself lost in depression's embrace,

Know that you're not alone in this desolate space.

There's light at the end, a glimmer of hope,

Embrace the journey, cling to the rope.

For you are a warrior, brave and profound,

With the power to rise, heal, and rebound.

In the face of adversity, you'll find your way,

Shedding the shadows, embracing a brighter day.

Embrace challenges to maintain a positive attitude with
determination

The journey is not easy, but it's a uphill battle

Poem

In the depths of despair, a soul did reside,

Bound by the chains of a job, I couldn't hide.

Passionate and driven, I once was so strong,

But now my spirit was silenced; my hope was gone.

Resigning from a job I loved, it tore them apart, my dreams
shattered, crushed by a heavy heart.

Depression consumed them, a relentless foe,

But little did I know I had the strength to grow.

In the darkness, they stumbled, searching for light,

A glimmer of hope to guide me through the night.

I faced my demons one by one,

Confronting my fears, I began to overcome.

I sought solace in nature, finding peace in its embrace,

Reconnecting with myself, finding my inner grace.

I surrounded myself with love and support,

Embracing my journey, with resilience, I fought.

Embrace challenges to maintain a positive attitude with
determination

The journey is not easy, but it's a uphill battle

I discovered new passions, uncharted and unknown,

Unlocking my potential, I began to own.

Through creativity and self-expression, I found release,

Writing, painting, singing, my soul found peace.

I sought therapy and counseling, a helping hand,

Learning coping mechanisms, I took a stand.

I cultivated self-care, nurturing my well-being,

Taking small steps forward, slowly, I began to start healing.

I learned to appreciate the present, letting go of the past,

Embracing the uncertainty, my strength was steadfast.

I found purpose in helping others, giving back,

Empathy and compassion on my new path, I did not lack.

Overcoming depression, a battle hard-fought,

I emerged stronger, with lessons dearly bought.

Resilient and determined, I rose from the ashes,

A testament to the power of my spirit's flashes.

Embrace challenges to maintain a positive attitude with
determination

The journey is not easy, but it's a uphill battle

So, if you find yourself in a similar plight,

Remember this journey, this story of light.

You have the strength within you to rise above,

To overcome the darkness, and rediscover love.

Embrace challenges to maintain a positive attitude with
determination

The journey is not easy, but it's a uphill battle

Poem

In the realm of words, where stories come alive,

There resides a passion that forever will thrive.

A writer's heart beats with ink and pen,

Creating worlds, weaving tales, again and again.

In the depths of imagination, a spark ignites,

A fire within, burning bright, day and night.

With every sentence, a new universe unfolds,

Characters dance, emotions untold.

Through the power of words, thoughts take flight,

Painting pictures, evoking feelings, pure delight.

With every stroke of the pen, a voice is found,

Expressing truths, in silence, profound.

In the sanctuary of solitude, the writer dwells,

Immersed in thoughts, the stories they tell.

They capture moments, both big and small,

Crafting narratives, to captivate us all.

Embrace challenges to maintain a positive attitude with
determination

The journey is not easy, but it's a uphill battle

Their words are a melody, a symphony of the soul,

Unveiling mysteries, making us whole.

They dive into depths, where others fear to tread,

Exploring emotions, both joy and dread.

Through poetry or prose, their hearts are laid bare,

Sharing their struggles, their joys, their despair.

They find solace in the rhythm, the flow,

A sanctuary for their thoughts to grow.

They breathe life into characters, both real and imagined,

Their stories, a tapestry, intricately patterned.

They challenge conventions, break through the norm,

Leaving an indelible mark, like a gathering storm.

Writing is their refuge, their truest expression,

A journey of discovery, a lifelong obsession.

With every word, they shape their reality,

Leaving a legacy, for generations to see.

Embrace challenges to maintain a positive attitude with
determination

The journey is not easy, but it's a uphill battle

So embrace your passion, let your voice be heard,

Tell the tales that dance within, like a bird.

For in the realm of writing, magic abounds,

Where dreams come alive, and love knows no bounds.

Embrace challenges to maintain a positive attitude with
determination

Everyday affirmation

I am feeling confident and ready to take on any challenges that come my way. I believe in my abilities and know that I have the strength and resilience to overcome any obstacles. I am not afraid to face my challenges head-on, and I am determined to push through and come out on top.

I have a positive mindset and believe that I can handle whatever life throws at me. I am not afraid to take risks and embrace the opportunities for growth and success that come with facing challenges. I trust in my capabilities and am confident in my ability to navigate through any difficulties that may arise.

I am determined to stand up to my challenges and continue to move forward with courage and determination. I am excited about the opportunities for personal and professional growth that come with overcoming challenges. I am ready to embrace the journey ahead and tackle any obstacles with confidence and resilience. Today, and every day, I am confident and ready to stand up to my challenges.

Only time can judge me

Today, I find solace in the phrase, "Only time can judge me." In a world filled with constant scrutiny and judgment from others, it is a reminder that the passage of

The journey is not easy, but it's a uphill battle

time holds the true measure of who I am and what I am capable of. The judgments of others may hold temporary power, but in the end, it is my actions, choices, and character that will stand the test of time.

In a society fueled by comparison and the need for validation, it is easy to become overwhelmed by the opinions and expectations of others. But today, I choose to release myself from the shackles of external judgment. I acknowledge and honor my worth and the unique path I am forging.

This phrase holds a profound meaning for me as I navigate through life's challenges and adversities. It serves as a reminder that I am the author of my story, and the judgments or opinions of others do not define me. Only time can truly reveal the depth of my growth, resilience, and strength.

It is important to remember that everyone has their own journey and experiences. We all possess scars, flaws, and imperfections, but it is how we navigate through them and grow that truly matters. When faced with moments of doubt or criticism, I will remind myself that it is only time that will provide a fair assessment of my true character and accomplishments.

By embracing this understanding, I am liberated from the burden of pleasing others or seeking constant approval. I can focus on being true to myself, pursuing my passions, and striving for personal growth. It is through this

Embrace challenges to maintain a positive attitude with determination

authenticity that I can cultivate a life that is meaningful and aligned with my values.

While the judgments of others may sting in the moment, I know that they hold no true power over me. I will rise above the noise and negativity, relying on the guidance of my own intuition and wisdom. I will trust that as time passes, my actions will speak louder than any external judgment, and my character will shine through.

This phrase reminds me to practice self-compassion and embrace patience. It encourages me to be kind to myself and understanding of my own journey. I will give myself the grace to make mistakes, learn from them, and continually evolve.

In the grand tapestry of life, only time can provide a fair and unbiased assessment of who I am and what I have accomplished. I will embrace this truth with gratitude, curiosity, and a commitment to living authentically and with integrity.

A journey of repentance

I find solace in the idea that repentance is my way of forgiving. As I reflect on the mistakes I have made and the harm I may have caused to others, I recognize the importance of acknowledging my faults and seeking forgiveness.

The journey is not easy, but it's a uphill battle

Repentance is not just a religious concept; it is a way of taking responsibility for my actions and truly understanding the impact they may have had on others. It requires humility, introspection, and a genuine desire for change. Through repentance, I acknowledge the pain I may have caused and make a commitment to rectify my wrongs.

The path of repentance is not easy. It takes courage to face my own flaws and mistakes. It requires me to confront uncomfortable truths and reflect upon the choices I have made. But amidst the discomfort, there is also growth and liberation. Repentance allows me to learn from my past and work towards becoming a better version of myself.

Through this process, I also recognize the power of forgiveness. By seeking forgiveness, not only from others but also from myself, I am letting go of the burden of guilt and shame. I am allowing myself the opportunity to heal and move forward.

It is important to note that forgiveness is not guaranteed. Each person I have hurt will have their own journey towards forgiveness, and it is not within my control. However, by sincerely repenting and taking action to amend my behavior and make reparations, I offer an opportunity for healing and reconciliation.

Repentance is a continuous practice. It is not a one-time event but a way of living and constantly striving to be better. It requires ongoing reflection, accountability, and a commitment to growth.

Embrace challenges to maintain a positive attitude with determination

Today, I embrace the power of repentance as my way of forgiving. I acknowledge my past mistakes and commit to learning from them and making amends. I offer my sincere apologies to those I have hurt and seek their forgiveness with humility and understanding.

Through this process, I also extend forgiveness to myself. I let go of self-blame and embrace the opportunity for growth and transformation. I recognize that I am capable of change and that my past does not define my future.

By embracing repentance as my way of forgiving, I walk a path of growth, compassion, and reconciliation. I am committed to making amends, seeking forgiveness, and continually striving to be the best version of myself.

My reaction to my circumstances

I am reminded of the profound impact my reactions have on shaping my experiences and how they allow me to embrace my circumstances with pride. It is easy to feel overwhelmed or disheartened when faced with challenging situations. However, I am choosing to embrace the power of my reactions and use them as a tool for growth, resilience, and empowerment.

I recognize that my reactions are within my control. While I may not have control over the circumstances themselves, I have complete authority over how I respond to them. This realization is both liberating and empowering. It means that, regardless of the challenges that come my

The journey is not easy, but it's a uphill battle

way, I have the ability to shape my own narrative and define my own path.

Instead of succumbing to negativity, self-pity, or resentment, I choose to approach my circumstances with a mindset of strength, positivity, and pride. I understand that my reactions can influence the outcome of a situation and impact not only myself but also those around me.

By choosing positivity and resilience in the face of adversity, I convey a message to others that I am capable and determined. Through my reactions, I can inspire and uplift those who may be going through similar circumstances, showing them that it is possible to overcome challenges and embrace their circumstances with pride.

I embrace the notion that my reactions are rooted in self-empowerment. Rather than allowing circumstances to define me, I define my response to them. I refuse to be a victim of my circumstances; instead, I use them as stepping stones for personal growth and self-discovery.

Embracing my circumstances with pride does not mean denying the difficulties or challenges they may bring. Instead, it means accepting them for what they are and finding the strength to navigate through them. It is acknowledging that every experience, both positive and negative, contributes to my personal growth and development.

I pledge to approach every challenge with a sense of determination, courage, and an unwavering belief in my

Embrace challenges to maintain a positive attitude with determination

abilities. I will not let setbacks define me, but rather I will derive strength from them. I choose to view obstacles as opportunities for growth and transformation, using my reactions as a means to propel me forward.

I embrace my circumstances with pride. I accept the challenges that come my way and recognize the power within me to shape my reactions. By choosing positivity, resilience, and determination, I pave the way for personal growth and fulfillment. I am proud of the person I am becoming through my reactions and the way I embrace my circumstances.

Discipline and creating boundaries

I am reflecting on the importance of disciplining myself and creating boundaries in order to break free from the grip of fear. Fear has often held me back from pursuing my dreams, taking risks, and living life to the fullest. However, I am committed to breaking this cycle and empowering myself to overcome fear through self-discipline and healthy boundaries.

Discipline is not about punishment or restriction; rather, it is about cultivating a sense of structure and focus within my life. By setting clear goals, prioritizing my time and energy, and adhering to a consistent routine, I am better equipped to face my fears head-on.

One aspect of disciplining myself is identifying the areas in which fear has the most control and asserting my power over them. It is crucial to recognize the limiting beliefs and negative self-talk that perpetuate fear and to replace them with empowering thoughts and affirmations. By consciously reframing my mindset, I can create a positive foundation from which to navigate life's challenges.

Creating boundaries is equally important in conquering fear. It involves identifying and acknowledging the people, situations, or circumstances that trigger fear within me. From there, I can establish healthy boundaries to protect my well-being and prevent fear from overwhelming my thoughts and actions.

Setting boundaries means having the courage to say no when something does not align with my values or brings unnecessary stress and fear into my life. It means surrounding myself with supportive and uplifting individuals who encourage and inspire me to step outside of my comfort zone.

I recognize that embarking on this journey requires patience, consistency, and self-compassion. Breaking free from fear is not an overnight process but a lifelong commitment to personal growth and self-discovery. There will be setbacks and moments of doubt, but I will stay committed to disciplining myself and establishing healthy boundaries.

I take the first steps towards disciplining myself and creating boundaries from fear. I commit to challenging myself, stepping out of my comfort zone, and embracing the unknown. I will replace self-doubt with self-belief, and I will

The journey is not easy, but it's a uphill battle

nurture a mindset of resilience, courage, and determination.

I understand that this journey will be challenging, but I am ready to face it head-on. I trust in my ability to grow and evolve, and I know that through discipline and boundary-setting, fear will no longer have a stronghold over my life.

A Journal on Regaining Moral When Feeling Sad

I am feeling incredibly down and unmotivated. It seems like everything is going wrong, and I can't seem to shake this feeling of sadness. I know that I need to regain my morale and find a way to lift my spirits. I've decided to start a journal to document my journey towards finding happiness again.

I've spent some time reflecting on the reasons behind my sadness. I've realized that I've been neglecting my self-care and haven't been practicing mindfulness. I've made a commitment to start taking better care of myself and to incorporate mindfulness practices into my daily routine.

I've reached out to a friend and opened up about how I've been feeling. It was incredibly helpful to have someone to talk to and share my thoughts and emotions with. I now realize the importance of seeking support from others when I'm feeling down.

Embrace challenges to maintain a positive attitude with determination

The journey is not easy, but it's a uphill battle

I've started engaging in activities that bring me joy and fulfillment. I've been going for walks in nature, listening to uplifting music, and practicing gratitude. These activities have helped to shift my mindset and bring a sense of positivity back into my life.

I've set some new goals for myself and have started taking small steps towards achieving them. Setting goals has given me a sense of purpose and direction, and I'm starting to feel more motivated and hopeful about the future.

I've been focusing on helping others and giving back to my community. Volunteering and acts of kindness have given me a sense of fulfillment and have helped to shift my focus away from my own sadness.

I'm feeling much more optimistic and hopeful than I was a week ago. Through self-care, seeking support, engaging in joyful activities, setting goals, and helping others, I've been able to regain my morale and find happiness again.

In conclusion, regaining morale when feeling sad is a journey that requires self-reflection, self-care, seeking support, engaging in joyful activities, setting goals, and helping others. It's important to remember that it's okay to feel sad, but there are steps we can take to lift our spirits and find happiness again.

Embrace challenges to maintain a positive attitude with determination

Dear Journal,

Today, I want to express my deep for writing. Writing has always been a way for me to channel my emotions onto paper. It allows me to explore new worlds, create unique characters, and share my ideas with others.

I always found solace the act of putting to paper or typing away on keyboard. The process of crafting a story or an article gives me a sense of purpose and fulfillment like nothing else can. Whether it's fiction, poetry, or non-fiction, writing has always been my chosen form of self-expression.

Every time I sit down to write, I am transported to a place where my imagination knows no bounds. It's a magical feeling to see words come to life on a blank page, forming sentences that convey exactly what I want to say. Writing allows me to connect with myself on a deeper level and helps me make sense of the world around me.

I am grateful for the gift of writing and the joy it brings me every day. It is a passion that I hold dear to my heart, and I know that I will continue to write for as long as I am able.

With love and gratitude,

The journey is not easy, but it's a uphill battle

Poem

In the pages of a journal, secrets unfold,

A sacred space where stories are told.

No matter what you're going through in life,

Writing your experiences can ease the strife.

When the weight of the world feels too much to bear,

Pour out your thoughts and release them into the air.

The blank pages await a canvas for your soul,

Where emotions can flow unfiltered and whole.

In the solitude of pen and paper, find solace,

Expressing your truth, finding your own compass.

For sometimes, sharing with others may be tough,

But in the journal's embrace, you've found enough.

Write your joys, your sorrows, your deepest fears,

Free yourself from the burden, let go of the tears.

In the privacy of those pages, you are free,

To explore your thoughts, to be authentically thee.

Embrace challenges to maintain a positive attitude with
determination

The journey is not easy, but it's a uphill battle

A journal is a companion, a trusted confidant,

Listening without judgment, offering solace and support.

Pouring your heart onto those pages, you see,

The power of self-reflection, the key to set you free.

Through self-thinking, you gain clarity and insight,

Unraveling the knots that keep you up at night.

You find patterns, uncover hidden truths,

Discovering strength within, like hidden roots.

So, remember, dear friend, in times of joy or strife,

Grab your pen, embrace the power of a journal in life.

Write your stories, your dreams, your pain,

For in those pages, your voice will forever remain.

Embrace challenges to maintain a positive attitude with
determination

The journey is not easy, but it's a uphill battle

Poem

With a heavy heart, I close this book,

A tale that I poured my soul into, every nook.

Regrets may linger, like shadows in the night,

But sometimes endings are necessary, to find the light.

Each chapter written, with passion and care,

Characters brought to life, moments we shared.

But now the time has come to bid farewell,

To let go of the story, to break the spell.

Regrets may haunt, like ghosts in the mind,

Questions unanswered, what ifs left behind.

But in every ending, there's a new beginning,

A chance to grow, to keep on spinning.

For every story has its own natural end,

A final page turned, a message to send.

Though it may be bittersweet, this closing line,

Remember, dear reader, it's not the final sign.

Embrace challenges to maintain a positive attitude with determination

The journey is not easy, but it's a uphill battle

For within these pages, a world was created,

A journey embarked upon, and memories elated.

The characters may rest, but their stories live on,

In the hearts of readers, long after they're gone.

So, with all regrets, I bid adieu,

To this book, this journey, that we once knew.

It may be the end, but it's not the final chapter,

For stories never truly end, they continue to capture.

And as the pages close, let us not forget,

The lessons learned, the emotions we met.

For even in endings, there's beauty to find,

And the hope of new beginnings, intertwined.

So, with all regrets, I put an end to this book,

But the memories and moments, forever I'll look.

For in the realm of stories, there's always more to tell,

And with open hearts, we'll write new tales, farewell.

Embrace challenges to maintain a positive attitude with
determination

Rising Above Discreditation

Today, I find myself reflecting on a recent experience that has left me feeling discredited and undermined. It's disheartening to have my efforts and abilities questioned, but I refuse to let this setback define me. Instead, I choose to rise above it and keep moving forward with unwavering strength.

In the face of discreditation, it's natural to feel a mix of emotions—anger, frustration, and self-doubt. However, I recognize that my worth and capabilities are not determined by the opinions of others. I am the author of my own story, and I refuse to let anyone else hold the pen.

It's important to remind myself that adversity is a part of life's journey. It provides an opportunity for growth and resilience. This discreditation may have momentarily shaken me, but it will not break me. I am stronger than the doubts and negativity that may surround me.

I choose to focus on the truth within myself—the knowledge, skills, and experiences that have shaped me into the person I am today. This setback is merely a hurdle in the path, not an insurmountable wall. I will rise above it with determination and grace.

In moments like this, it's crucial to surround myself with a support network of family, friends, and mentors who believe in me and uplift me. Their encouragement and belief

The journey is not easy, but it's a uphill battle

in my abilities serve as a constant reminder that I am capable and deserving of success.

As I navigate this challenging time, I will also practice self-care and self-compassion. I will take time to nurture my mental and emotional well-being, acknowledging that it's okay to feel vulnerable but not let it consume me. I will engage in activities that bring me joy, whether it's writing, painting, or spending time in nature, to replenish my spirit and regain my confidence.

Moving forward, I will channel this discreditation into motivation. It fuels my determination to prove myself, not to others, but to myself. I will continue to pursue my goals and aspirations with unwavering passion and resilience. I will use this experience as a catalyst for growth, pushing myself beyond my comfort zone and embracing new opportunities.

In conclusion, although discreditation may have momentarily dimmed my light, I refuse to let it extinguish my fire. I am strong, capable, and deserving of success. I will rise above this setback, armed with self-belief and unwavering determination. Onward I go, with my head held high and my spirit unyielding.

Holding Others Accountable for Policy Adherence

Embrace challenges to maintain a positive attitude with determination

The journey is not easy, but it's a uphill battle

Today, I find myself reflecting on a recent experience where I had to hold others accountable for not following established policies. It was a challenging situation that required courage, assertiveness, and a commitment to upholding the standards that have been set. Although the outcome may have been difficult, it was a necessary step toward ensuring fairness, integrity, and the overall success of the organization.

Initially, I felt a sense of hesitation and apprehension about addressing the issue. The fear of confrontation and potential backlash weighed heavily on my mind. However, I reminded myself of the importance of maintaining a work environment that operates within the boundaries of established policies and regulations. I understood that by holding others accountable, I was not only advocating for the organization's best interests but also for the well-being and success of my colleagues.

The process of addressing the non-compliance was not easy. It required thorough investigation, gathering evidence, and having open and honest conversations with the individuals involved. It was essential to approach the situation with objectivity, fairness, and respect, ensuring that each person had an opportunity to provide their perspective.

As I progressed through the process, I faced resistance and pushback from some individuals. It was disheartening to see the negative reactions and attempts to deflect responsibility. However, I remained steadfast in my

Embrace challenges to maintain a positive attitude with determination

commitment to upholding the policies and ensuring accountability. I maintained a calm and composed demeanor, relying on facts and clear communication to address any misconceptions or misunderstandings.

In the end, the outcome of holding others accountable varied. Some individuals acknowledged their mistakes and took responsibility for their actions. They expressed a commitment to rectifying the situation and adhering to the policies moving forward. This outcome provided a sense of relief and optimism, as it demonstrated the potential for growth and improvement within the organization.

On the other hand, there were individuals who remained resistant and unwilling to accept accountability. Despite my best efforts to communicate the importance of policy adherence, they continued to challenge the consequences and attempt to bypass the established protocols. This outcome was disappointing, as it highlighted the need for further action and potentially more extensive interventions to ensure compliance.

Reflecting on this experience, I recognize the importance of perseverance and unwavering commitment to upholding policies. Holding others accountable is not always an easy task, but it is a necessary one. It ensures fairness, integrity, and the overall success of the organization. It also fosters a culture of trust and respect, where everyone is held to the same standards and expectations.

Embrace challenges to maintain a positive attitude with determination

The journey is not easy, but it's a uphill battle

Moving forward, I will continue to prioritize accountability and advocate for policy adherence. I will approach these situations with empathy and understanding, recognizing that change and growth take time. I will remain steadfast in upholding the policies that have been put in place, knowing that my efforts contribute to a positive and thriving work environment.

Taking in consideration

When facing bad news or a difficult situation, it's important to remember that it's okay to feel upset or disappointed. Allow yourself to acknowledge your emotions and process them in a healthy way. Once you've given yourself time to feel your feelings, try to shift your perspective towards finding a positive outlook or solution.

One approach is to focus on what you can control and take proactive steps to improve the situation. Look for opportunities to learn and grow from the experience, and consider how you can use it as a chance to develop resilience and strength. Remember that setbacks are a natural part of life, and by facing them with a positive attitude, you can set yourself up for a better outcome in the long run.

Absolutely! Your daily journal can serve as a valuable for finding motivation, inspiration, encouragement, and strength. By revisiting the lessons and messages within your journal, you can remind yourself of your own wisdom and

Embrace challenges to maintain a positive attitude with determination

experiences that have helped you overcome challenges in the past. Use your daily as a tool to boost your confidence, fuel your determination, and support your growth during difficult times. Remember, you have the power within you to conquer any obstacle that comes your way.

A positive-mindset is the key that opens the doors of happiness leading to a field where the flowers of serenity and personal fulfillment grow. When life gets more difficult, you have to find the strength within yourself to still believe and embrace life-disappointment.

Knowing Distress to Appreciate Love

Today, I find myself reflecting on the profound realization that experiencing distress can deepen our appreciation for love. It is in moments of hardship and emotional turmoil that we truly come to understand the value and significance of love in our lives.

Distress has a way of shaking us to our core, leaving us vulnerable and in need of support. It can take various forms, whether it be heartbreak, loss, or personal struggles. In these moments, it may feel as though love is distant or elusive, but it is during these times that its importance becomes abundantly clear.

When we experience distress, we become acutely aware of the impact that love has on our well-being. It is in the absence of love, or the yearning for it, that we recognize its power to heal, comfort, and uplift us. Love has the ability

The journey is not easy, but it's a uphill battle

to mend our broken hearts, provide solace in our darkest moments, and remind us of our inherent worth.

Distress teaches us to appreciate the love that surrounds us, both from others and within ourselves. It highlights the significance of the connections we have with our loved ones, reminding us to cherish and nurture those relationships. It prompts us to express our gratitude and affection to those who have supported us through difficult times.

Furthermore, distress teaches us the importance of self-love and self-care. It reminds us that we are deserving of love, compassion, and kindness, especially during times of struggle. It encourages us to prioritize our own well-being and cultivate a loving relationship with ourselves.

Just as darkness allows us to fully appreciate the light, distress enables us to recognize and value the love that exists in our lives. It serves as a powerful reminder that love is not to be taken for granted but rather cherished and nurtured.

Moving forward, I will strive to carry this awareness with me, even in times of joy and contentment. I will consciously cultivate a deep appreciation for the love that surrounds me, expressing gratitude and affection to those who have touched my life. I will also prioritize self-love and self-care, recognizing that my own well-being is essential for experiencing and sharing love with others.

Embrace challenges to maintain a positive attitude with determination

The journey is not easy, but it's a uphill battle

In conclusion, distress serves as a teacher, guiding us toward a profound appreciation for love. Through its trials and tribulations, we come to understand the transformative power of love in our lives. May we embrace this knowledge and carry it with us, fostering a deeper connection to both the love within us and the love that surrounds us.

Embracing the Beauty of Solitude

Today, I find myself reflecting on the deep appreciation I have for solitude and its essential role in my overall wellbeing. Solitude, to me, is more than just being alone—it is a sacred space where I can reconnect with myself, find inner peace, and recharge my spirit.

In the bustling world we live in, it is easy to get caught up in the constant noise and distractions that surround us. Solitude offers me a respite from the external chaos and allows me to turn inward, to listen to the whispers of my own thoughts and emotions. It is in this stillness that I discover a sense of clarity and self-awareness that is vital for my personal growth.

Solitude provides me with an opportunity to reflect and introspect. It is during these moments of solitude that I can truly explore my own thoughts, dreams, and desires without any external influences or judgments. I can delve deep into the depths of my being, uncovering hidden truths and gaining a better understanding of who I am and what I truly need.

Embrace challenges to maintain a positive attitude with determination

The journey is not easy, but it's a uphill battle

In solitude, I find solace and tranquility. It is a time when I can fully embrace my own company, free from the pressures of social expectations or the need to constantly engage with others. I can indulge in activities that bring me joy, whether it's reading a book, taking a walk in nature, or simply sitting in silence. These moments of solitude nourish my soul and rejuvenate my spirit.

Moreover, solitude allows me the space to recharge and replenish my energy. It gives me the opportunity to disconnect from the demands of the outside world and focus on self-care. In solitude, I can nurture my physical, emotional, and mental well-being, ensuring that I am able to show up fully in all aspects of my life.

While solitude may be seen by some as isolating or lonely, I have come to appreciate its transformative power. It is in the moments of solitude that I am able to cultivate a deep sense of self-love and acceptance. I learn to enjoy my own company and find contentment in the present moment, embracing the beauty of solitude as an essential part of my wellbeing.

Moving forward, I will continue to prioritize and cherish moments of solitude in my life. I will create an intentional space to disconnect from the noise of the world and reconnect with myself. Whether it's through meditation, journaling, or simply finding moments of quiet, I will honor the importance of solitude in nurturing my well-being.

Embrace challenges to maintain a positive attitude with determination

In conclusion, solitude is a gift that I gratefully embrace. It is in the stillness and quietude that I find a sense of peace, self-discovery, and rejuvenation. Solitude is not a state of loneliness but a sacred space where I can fully connect with myself and cultivate a deep sense of well-being.

Embracing the Flow of Thoughts

Today, I find myself reflecting on the idea that controlling my thoughts may be counterproductive. Throughout my life, I have often believed that I needed to have complete control over my thoughts, constantly striving to direct them in a specific direction. However, I now realize that this approach may hinder my growth and limit my ability to embrace the full range of human experiences.

Thoughts are like wild rivers, flowing freely and unpredictably. They have a life of their own, emerging from the depths of our consciousness without our conscious control. Instead of trying to control and suppress these thoughts, I am learning to embrace them with curiosity and mindfulness.

For many years, I believed that controlling my thoughts was a means to maintain order and stability in my mind. I saw it as a way to protect myself from negative or intrusive thoughts. However, I now understand that by trying to control my thoughts, I am actually denying myself

The journey is not easy, but it's a uphill battle

the opportunity to explore and understand the complexities of my own mind.

When I allow my thoughts to flow naturally, without judgment or resistance, I create space for self-discovery and growth. I can observe the patterns and themes that arise, gaining insight into my fears, desires, and beliefs. In this process, I am able to cultivate self-awareness and develop a deeper understanding of myself.

Moreover, by embracing the flow of thoughts, I am better equipped to navigate the challenges and uncertainties of life. I can acknowledge and accept the thoughts that arise, whether they are positive or negative, without being consumed by them. This acceptance allows me to respond to life's circumstances with greater resilience and adaptability.

Rather than controlling my thoughts, I am learning to cultivate a gentle presence and non-attachment towards them. I am practicing mindfulness, observing my thoughts without judgment, and allowing them to come and go like passing clouds in the sky. This practice nurtures a sense of inner peace and freedom as I release the need to control and manipulate my thoughts.

Moving forward, I will continue to embrace the flow of thoughts and let go of the desire for control. I will cultivate self-compassion, acknowledging that thoughts are a natural part of being human. I will engage in practices that support mindfulness and self-reflection, allowing me to

Embrace challenges to maintain a positive attitude with determination

navigate the ebb and flow of thoughts with grace and openness.

In conclusion, I am learning that controlling my thoughts may be counterproductive. Instead, I choose to embrace the flow of thoughts with curiosity and mindfulness. By doing so, I open myself up to self-discovery, growth, and a greater sense of inner peace.

Choosing to Respond to Emotions

Today, I find myself reflecting on the profound realization that responding to my emotions is a choice. Throughout my life, I often believed that my emotions controlled me, dictating my actions and reactions. However, I now understand that I have the power to choose how I respond to my emotions, ultimately shaping my experiences and well-being.

Emotions are a natural part of being human. They arise within us, triggered by various internal and external factors. While we cannot control the initial surge of emotions, we can choose how we respond to them. This awareness empowers me to navigate the complexities of my emotions with intention and mindfulness.

In the past, I may have allowed my emotions to dictate my actions without considering the consequences. I would react impulsively, driven by anger, sadness, or fear. However, I now recognize that this reactive response was not serving my highest good. It often led to regret, damaged relationships, and a sense of powerlessness.

By realizing that responding to my emotions is a choice, I am now able to approach them with greater awareness and understanding. I can pause, take a deep breath, and consciously decide how I want to respond. This choice allows me to detach from the immediate intensity of the emotion and consider the most effective and constructive course of action.

Choosing to respond to my emotions also means taking responsibility for my own well-being. I understand that my emotions are valid and deserve acknowledgment. However, I do not let them define me or dictate my entire experience. Instead, I actively work towards cultivating emotional intelligence and resilience, allowing me to navigate life's challenges with grace and composure.

In this journey, I have learned the importance of self-reflection and self-care. By taking the time to understand the underlying causes of my emotions and addressing them with compassion, I can respond from a place of authenticity and alignment with my values. I prioritize self-care practices that promote emotional well-being, such as meditation, journaling, and seeking support from loved ones or professionals when needed.

Moving forward, I will continue to embrace the understanding that responding to my emotions is a choice. I will commit to cultivating emotional intelligence and resilience, allowing me to respond to my emotions with clarity and wisdom. I will approach each emotion as an opportunity for self-growth and self-discovery, knowing that I have the power to shape my experiences and create a life of fulfillment and balance.

In conclusion, I am grateful for the realization that responding to my emotions is a choice. This awareness empowers me to navigate the complexities of my emotions with intention and mindfulness. By making conscious choices, I can cultivate emotional well-being and create a life in alignment with my truest self.

Transforming Adversity into Inspiration

Life has a way of throwing unexpected curveballs, leaving us feeling overwhelmed and lost in the midst of chaos. But what if we could turn our mess into a message? What if we could find purpose and meaning in the midst of our struggles? This is the remarkable journey that I embarked upon, transforming my own personal mess into a powerful message of inspiration and hope.

Embracing the Mess:

Like many others, I have faced my fair share of challenges, setbacks, and failures. Life seemed like a never-ending series of hurdles, and I often found myself questioning my purpose and worth. But instead of succumbing to despair, I made a conscious decision to embrace my mess. I refused to let it define me, and I began to see it as an opportunity for growth and transformation.

Finding Lessons in Failure:

Failure is often seen as a reflection of our shortcomings, a sign that we are not capable or worthy. However, I chose to view failure as a valuable teacher, guiding me toward self-discovery and personal development. Each setback became an opportunity to learn, adapt, and grow stronger. I recognized that failure was not the end but a stepping stone on the path to success.

Seeking Support and Healing:

Transforming my message into a message required me to seek support and prioritize my own healing. I surrounded myself with a network of loved ones, mentors, and professionals who provided guidance, encouragement, and a listening ear. Through therapy, self-reflection, and self-care practices, I began to heal from past wounds and cultivate a deeper understanding of myself.

Discovering Purpose:

In the midst of my mess, I began to uncover a sense of purpose. I realized that my experiences, struggles, and triumphs could serve as a source of inspiration for others.

Embrace challenges to maintain a positive attitude with determination

The journey is not easy, but it's a uphill battle

By sharing my story, I could offer hope, encouragement, and guidance to those facing similar challenges. My mess became the catalyst for my message, driving me to make a difference in the lives of others.

Sharing the Message:

I took the brave step of sharing my journey, turning my mess into a message for the world to hear. Through writing, speaking engagements, and other creative outlets, I shared my story with authenticity and vulnerability. I aimed to inspire others to embrace their own mess and find strength in their vulnerabilities. By sharing my message, I hoped to ignite a spark of hope and resilience in those who needed it most.

Impact and Transformation:

Witnessing the impact of my message has been incredibly fulfilling. I have received messages from individuals who found solace and inspiration in my story. Knowing that I have made a positive difference in someone else's life has fueled my passion to continue sharing my message. I am humbled by the opportunity to turn my mess into a force for good and create a ripple effect of transformation in the lives of others.

Conclusion:

Embrace challenges to maintain a positive attitude with determination

The journey is not easy, but it's a uphill battle

Turning our mess into a message is a courageous and transformative journey. By embracing our struggles, learning from failure, seeking support, and sharing our stories, we can inspire and uplift others who may be going through similar challenges. Through our mess, we can find purpose, meaning, and a profound sense of fulfillment. So, let us embrace our mess, transform it into a powerful message, and make a lasting impact on the world.

Embrace challenges to maintain a positive attitude with determination

Narrative

"In life, we all face challenges and obstacles that can sometimes feel overwhelming. It's easy to get caught up in negative thoughts and emotions, but it's important to remember that you have the power to change your mindset and overcome any adversity that comes your way.

This book is a guide to help you tap into your inner strength and resilience, providing practical tips and exercises to help you navigate through life's ups and downs. By learning how to cultivate a positive mindset, set goals, and practice self-care, you can empower yourself to live a fulfilling and meaningful life.

Remember, you are capable of achieving great things and overcoming any obstacle that stands in your way. With the right tools and mindset, you can create the life you truly desire. So, let's embark on this journey together and unlock your full potential."

What inspired me to write "The Journey Is Not Easy, But It's an Uphill Battle"?

The inspiration behind this book came from my personal experiences and observations of people facing various obstacles and challenges in life. I noticed that despite the difficulties, many individuals demonstrated incredible resilience and determination in their efforts to overcome adversity. That resilience fueled my desire to write a book that could motivate and encourage others, reminding them that the journey may be tough, but it is also where true growth and triumph lie.

That's incredibly inspiring. I can tell you more about the central message and themes explored in the book!!

"The Journey Is Not Easy, But It's an Uphill Battle" is a tribute to resilience and the indomitable human spirit. Through personal anecdotes, uplifting stories, and engaging insights, I guide readers on a reflective journey that encourages them to embrace the challenges they face. The book addresses themes such as courage, self-belief, perseverance, and the profound impact of adopting a positive mindset. It offers practical tools, strategies, and exercises to help readers navigate their own uphill battles with newfound strength and determination.

My book is like a truly transformative read. How do I envision this book impacting readers' lives?

What sets my book apart is its authentic and relatable approach. I draw from personal experiences and captivating narratives to connect with readers on a deep emotional level. Additionally, "The Journey Is Not Easy, But It's an Uphill Battle" provides practical guidance and exercises throughout, enabling readers to truly engage with the material and implement the strategies in their own lives. It's not just a book to read; it's an immersive experience that empowers readers to take action and embrace their own uphill battles.

My book is truly compelling. "The Journey Is Not Easy, But It's an Uphill Battle"?

"The Journey Is Not Easy, But It's an Uphill Battle" is available for purchase on popular online retailers such as Amazon and Barnes & Noble. It's available in both paperback and ebook formats, ensuring readers can access it conveniently.

I truly believe that "The Journey Is Not Easy, But It's an Uphill Battle" will touch the hearts and minds of readers worldwide. It has been a pleasure having you with us.

My ultimate goal with this book is to reignite the flame of hope within readers' hearts. By sharing stories of individuals who faced seemingly insurmountable obstacles and triumphed against the odds, I aim to inspire readers to cultivate their own resilience and strength. I want readers to realize that their struggles do not define them but rather provide a platform for personal growth and transformation. This book serves as a roadmap, arming readers with invaluable insights and empowering them to embrace their own journeys, no matter how challenging they may seem.

It has been an honor to share my book and its message with your audience. I hope it inspires many to embrace their journeys and conquer their uphill battles with unwavering determination.

Narrator: Introducing a book that will ignite your spirit, empower your mind, and inspire your journey. Get ready to embrace the uphill battle and triumph in your own

The journey is not easy, but it's a uphill battle

unique way as we unveil "Embrace the Uphill Battle and Triumph in Your Journey." Life is a series of ups and downs, a rollercoaster of adversity and triumph.

Embrace challenges to maintain a positive attitude with determination

The Power of Hope

In the depths of despair and darkness, there exists a powerful force that has the ability to transform lives and bring about miracles. This force is hope. It is the flickering flame that lights up the darkest of nights, guiding us towards a brighter tomorrow. Hope is the belief that better days are ahead, that there is purpose and meaning even in the midst of chaos and uncertainty.

When all seems lost and the world feels heavy on our shoulders, hope whispers to us to keep going, to not give up. It is the gentle voice that reminds us that we are capable of overcoming any obstacle, no matter how insurmountable it may seem. Hope is the fuel that ignites our passion, our resilience, and our determination to persevere in the face of adversity.

In times of despair, hope is our lifeline. It is what sustains us through the storms of life, guiding us towards the light at the end of the tunnel. It is the anchor that keeps us grounded when everything around us feels like it is falling apart. Hope is not just a fleeting feeling; it is a conscious choice that we make every day to believe in the possibility of a better future.

Hope is not passive; it is an active force that propels us forward, urging us to take action and create the future we desire. It is the spark that ignites creativity, innovation, and change. With hope in our hearts, we can move mountains, break barriers, and achieve the seemingly impossible.

In a world filled with chaos, hardship, and despair, hope is our greatest ally. It is what gives us the strength to face each day with courage and resilience. It is the unwavering faith that tomorrow can be better than today, no matter how dark the present may seem.

So as we navigate the challenges and uncertainties of life, let us hold on to hope with unwavering conviction. Let us embrace its power to uplift us, inspire us, and guide us towards a future filled with promise and possibility. For in the darkest of nights, hope is the beacon that lights our way, reminding us that there is always light at the end of the tunnel.

Hope is the thread that weaves through the tapestry of our lives, connecting us to our innermost selves and to others. It is the bridge that spans the gap between despair and joy, between fear and courage. When we hold onto hope, we become beacons of light for others, showing them that there is always a way forward, no matter how bleak the circumstances may appear.

Hope is not a fleeting emotion; it is a steadfast companion that walks beside us on our journey through life. It is the voice that whispers words of encouragement in our ears when all seems lost. It is the silent strength that carries us through the darkest of nights and the fiercest of storms.

The journey is not easy, but it's a uphill battle

In the tapestry of human experience, hope is the golden thread that shines brightest, illuminating the path ahead and reminding us that we are not alone. It is the eternal flame that burns in our hearts, sustaining us through the trials and tribulations of life. Hope is the compass that guides us through the darkness, leading us towards a future filled with possibilities and promise.

So let us hold onto hope with unwavering faith and courage. Let us nurture it, cherish it, and let it grow within us until it becomes an unshakable foundation upon which we build our dreams and aspirations. For in the vast expanse of the universe, hope is the force that binds us all together, reminding us of our shared humanity and our collective potential to create a better world for ourselves and future generations.

Embrace challenges to maintain a positive attitude with determination

Nurturing Seeds of Optimism

Nurturing Seeds of Optimism

In a world where negativity often seems to hold sway, the practice of nurturing seeds of optimism becomes not just a luxury but a necessity for mental and emotional well-being. Amidst the chaos and uncertainty that surrounds us, it can be tempting to succumb to pessimism and despair. However, the power of optimism lies in its ability to not only see the light at the end of the tunnel but to actively seek out and create that light.

Optimism is not a passive state of mind but an active choice to believe in the possibility of better outcomes despite the challenges we face. It is the unwavering faith that amidst the darkness, there exists a flicker of hope waiting to be nourished and grown into a beacon of light.

One of the most potent ways to cultivate optimism is through the practice of gratitude. Gratitude is a transformative force that shifts our focus from what is lacking in our lives to what is abundant. By acknowledging and appreciating the blessings, big and small, that surround us, we pave the way for a mindset that is rooted in positivity and resilience.

Gratitude is not just a fleeting feeling of thankfulness but a practice that requires consistency and mindfulness. Keeping a gratitude journal, where we jot down three things we are grateful for each day, can significantly impact our overall outlook on life. This simple act of acknowledging the good can have a ripple effect, helping us navigate challenges with a sense of perspective and hope.

Furthermore, surrounding ourselves with a supportive community can be a powerful antidote to pessimism. The people we choose to spend our time with can either uplift us or drag us down. Cultivating relationships with individuals who radiate positivity and encouragement can boost our spirits and help us stay grounded in times of adversity. Sharing our struggles with those who genuinely care not only lessens the burden but also strengthens our sense of interconnectedness and belonging.

Taking care of our physical and mental well-being is also integral to nurturing optimism. Engaging in activities that bring us joy, practicing self-compassion, and prioritizing rest are all essential components of maintaining a positive mindset. Our bodies and minds are intricately connected, and when we neglect one, the other inevitably suffers. By honoring our holistic well-being, we lay the foundation for a resilient spirit that can weather any storm.

In the garden of life, optimism is the seed that, when nurtured with intention and care, blossoms into a tapestry of possibilities and opportunities. It is a choice we make every day, a commitment to seeing the world through the lens of hope and possibility. As we tend to these seeds of optimism, we not only cultivate a brighter future for ourselves but also sow the seeds of positivity in the world around us.

Embracing Uncertainty with Courage

In the depths of uncertainty, where the shadows of the unknown loom large and the whispers of doubt echo through the corridors of the mind, courage is the beacon that guides us forward. It is the steady pulse that beats within us, urging us to step boldly into the murky waters of the future, knowing that we have the strength to navigate whatever storms may come our way.

Uncertainty is a natural part of life, a reminder that the only constant is change. It is a test of our resilience, a challenge to our beliefs and perceptions. In the face of uncertainty, we are forced to confront our deepest fears and insecurities, to question our very sense of self. It is in these moments of doubt and confusion that our true character is revealed, where we have the opportunity to rise above our limitations and embrace the unknown with open arms.

Courage is not something that can be summoned at will, like a flick of a switch. It is a journey, a process of growth and transformation. It is the willingness to take a leap of faith, even when the path ahead is shrouded in darkness. It is the choice to face our fears head-on, to confront the demons that haunt us and emerge stronger on the other side.

When we embrace uncertainty with courage, we open ourselves up to a world of possibilities. We become more attuned to the rhythms of life, more in tune with the ebb and flow of the universe. We learn to trust in the wisdom of the unknown, knowing that there is a higher purpose at play, guiding us towards our true destiny.

So, as you stand on the precipice of uncertainty, remember to breathe deeply and trust in your inner strength. Know that you are capable of navigating the twists and turns of the unknown, with courage as your compass and resilience as your anchor. Embrace the uncertainty with an open heart and a fearless spirit, knowing that it is through facing our fears that we truly come alive.

In the silence of uncertainty, there is an opportunity for introspection, for growth and self-discovery. It is in these moments of pause, of contemplation, that we can truly understand the depth of our own courage. We unearth hidden reserves of strength and resilience, tapping into a wellspring of determination that empowers us to face the unknown with grace and dignity.

As we walk the tightrope between fear and bravery, uncertainty becomes a canvas on which we paint the colors of our dreams and aspirations. It is a blank slate, a realm of infinite possibilities waiting to be explored. With each step we take into the unknown, we shed our old skins and emerge as warriors of the soul, ready to conquer whatever challenges lie ahead.

Let uncertainty be your ally, not your adversary. Embrace its mysteries and complexities with an open mind and a willing heart. For it is in the crucible of uncertainty that we forge our truest selves, refining our spirits and

The journey is not easy, but it's a uphill battle

honing our instincts until we shine with the brilliance of a thousand suns. Embrace the journey, dear traveler, for the path of uncertainty is the path of transformation.

Finding Light in Dark Moments

In the depths of despair, where shadows linger and hope feels like a distant memory, there exists a profound truth that transcends the darkness. It is the recognition that within each of us lies an unyielding spark of light, a force that defies the gloom and radiates with unwavering strength.

In the crucible of adversity, this internal light flickers, sometimes imperceptible amidst the turmoil and chaos of life's trials. Yet, it remains steadfast, a beacon of resilience that guides us through the darkest moments. It is a testament to the human spirit, a reminder of our inherent capacity to endure and overcome even the most formidable challenges.

The quest to find light in dark moments is not merely a passive pursuit; it demands a conscious effort to cultivate awareness and seek out sources of positivity and inspiration amidst the gloom. It beckons us to look beyond the shadows and embrace the moments of beauty and joy that punctuate the somber landscape of despair.

Through the practice of mindfulness and self-care, we nurture this inner light, allowing it to grow and illuminate even the bleakest of circumstances. It is a

Embrace challenges to maintain a positive attitude with determination

The journey is not easy, but it's a uphill battle

practice of self-compassion, of acknowledging our pain and suffering with kindness and understanding, recognizing that vulnerability is not a weakness but a gateway to resilience.

Gratitude becomes a potent ally in our quest for light, reminding us of the blessings that grace our lives even in the midst of turmoil. It is a conscious choice to shift our focus from the darkness that envelops us to the flickers of hope and love that surround us, nurturing a sense of connection and purpose that sustains us through adversity.

In the labyrinthine depths of despair, where shadows loom large and despair threatens to consume us, the light within us beckons, a silent but potent force that reminds us of our capacity for strength and renewal. It is a reminder that even in the darkest moments, the seeds of hope and resilience lie dormant, waiting to blossom with the promise of a new dawn.

As we navigate the treacherous waters of despair, we realize that the journey towards light is not a linear path but a series of ebbs and flows, highs and lows. We encounter setbacks and obstacles that test our resolve, pushing us to the brink of despair. Yet, it is in these moments of darkness that the light within us shines brightest, a glimmer of hope that refuses to be extinguished.

Through the darkness, we discover the depth of our resilience, the wellspring of strength that lies within us, waiting to be tapped. It is a revelation that transforms our perception of despair, turning it from a force that overwhelms us to a catalyst for growth and transformation.

Embrace challenges to maintain a positive attitude with determination

In the crucible of suffering, we emerge stronger, wiser, and more attuned to the richness of life's tapestry.

And so, we embrace the darkness not as a foe to be vanquished but as a companion on the journey towards light. We learn to dance with the shadows, to find solace in the stillness, and to glean wisdom from the depths of despair. For it is in the moments of darkness that we discover the true power of our inner light, a force that transcends all obstacles and illuminates our path with unwavering clarity and grace.

Cultivating Gratitude in Daily Life

In the intricate tapestry of our existence, the practice of gratitude emerges as a beacon of light, illuminating the shadows of doubt and discontent. It is a transformative force that transcends the confines of time and space, weaving a thread of connection between the past, present, and future. Through the lens of gratitude, we embark on a journey of self-discovery and realization, uncovering hidden treasures in the most unexpected places.

Gratitude is not merely a fleeting emotion or obligatory courtesy; it is a profound state of being that resonates at the core of our humanity. It is a recognition of the interconnectedness of all things, a humble acknowledgment of the gifts that grace our lives in myriad forms. When we cultivate a heart steeped in gratitude, we

The journey is not easy, but it's a uphill battle

align ourselves with the universal rhythm of abundance, inviting blessings to flow effortlessly into our lives.

Numerous studies have affirmed the transformative power of gratitude, revealing its profound effects on our mental, emotional, and physical well-being. By shifting our focus from scarcity to sufficiency, from lack to abundance, we nurture a mindset that is attuned to the inherent goodness and beauty that surrounds us. This shift in perspective opens the floodgates of positivity, enriching our lived experience with a depth of satisfaction and contentment that transcends material wealth.

The practice of keeping a gratitude journal serves as a sacred sanctuary for our reflections and revelations, a space where we can pause and ponder the countless blessings that grace our lives each day. Through the simple act of recording three things we are grateful for, we cultivate a habit of mindfulness that tunes us into the symphony of gratitude playing in the background of our existence. In the gentle rhythm of this practice, we find solace and inspiration, grounding ourselves in the richness of the present moment.

Expressing gratitude to others becomes a natural extension of our practice, a way of paying homage to the interconnected web of relationships that sustains and nurtures us. When we acknowledge and appreciate the contributions of those who have touched our lives, we deepen our bonds of connection and foster a sense of communal reciprocity that enriches our shared human

Embrace challenges to maintain a positive attitude with determination

experience. In the exchange of gratitude, we find not only an outpouring of appreciation but a deepening of empathy, understanding, and love.

As we continue to cultivate a spirit of gratitude in our daily lives, we awaken to the profound interconnectedness of all beings and all things. We realize that gratitude is not just a sentiment but a way of being, a way of seeing, a way of living in harmony with the abundant gifts that surround us. In the infinite expanse of gratitude, we discover a universe of possibility and potential, where every moment is pregnant with the promise of grace and beauty.

Overcoming Obstacles with Resilience

In life, obstacles are inevitable. They come in various forms – from personal challenges to external circumstances beyond our control. However, what truly matters is how we respond to these obstacles. Resilience is the key to overcoming adversity and emerging stronger on the other side.

Resilience is not about avoiding obstacles or pretending they don't exist. It's about facing them head-on with courage and determination. It's about believing in your ability to bounce back from setbacks and move forward despite the challenges that come your way.

When faced with obstacles, it's important to acknowledge your feelings and emotions. Allow yourself to experience frustration, fear, or disappointment, but don't let these emotions paralyze you. Instead, use them as fuel to push through the obstacle and find a way to overcome it.

Resilience also involves developing a positive mindset. Instead of dwelling on the difficulties you face, focus on the opportunities for growth and learning that come with overcoming obstacles. See setbacks as temporary roadblocks rather than insurmountable barriers.

Furthermore, it's essential to build a support system of friends, family, or mentors who can offer guidance and encouragement during challenging times. Lean on these relationships for strength and perspective when you feel overwhelmed by obstacles.

Remember, resilience is a skill that can be cultivated and strengthened over time. By facing obstacles with perseverance, adaptability, and a positive outlook, you can navigate life's challenges with grace and emerge stronger than ever before.

In cultivating resilience, it's also crucial to practice self-care and self-compassion. Taking care of your physical, mental, and emotional well-being lays a solid foundation for facing obstacles with resilience. Make time for activities that bring you joy and relaxation, prioritize healthy habits, and be gentle with yourself during tough times.

Additionally, staying adaptable and open-minded is key to navigating obstacles successfully. Being willing to adjust your plans, try new approaches, and seek alternative solutions can help you overcome unexpected challenges more effectively.

Moreover, embracing a growth mindset can further enhance your resilience. Viewing obstacles as opportunities for personal growth and development can shift your perspective from seeing them as roadblocks to seeing them as stepping stones on your journey toward success.

Ultimately, cultivating resilience is an ongoing journey that requires practice, patience, and perseverance. By building your inner strength, harnessing your support network, and staying committed to your personal growth, you can not only overcome obstacles but also thrive in the face of adversity.

The journey is not easy, but it's a uphill battle

Synopsis:

"Life's Uphill Battle" is an inspiring and heartfelt book that explores the challenges, setbacks, and triumphs that shape our journey through life. Through a collection of personal stories, insightful reflections, and practical advice, the book offers a powerful message of resilience, hope, and the strength of the human spirit.

In this poignant memoir, I share their own experiences of navigating the ups and downs of life. From overcoming personal hardships and facing unexpected obstacles to pursuing dreams and finding purpose, they provide a raw and honest account of the struggles that many of us can relate to.

The book highlights the reality that life is not always easy. It acknowledges the hardships we encounter along the way, whether it be financial struggles, relationship difficulties, health issues, or the pressure to meet societal expectations. However, instead of dwelling on the challenges, the author emphasizes the importance of embracing these obstacles as opportunities for growth and transformation.

Throughout the book, I share valuable insights and practical strategies for overcoming adversity. They offer guidance on developing resilience, cultivating a positive mindset, and finding inner strength during difficult times. Drawing from their own experiences, they provide relatable

Embrace challenges to maintain a positive attitude with determination

The journey is not easy, but it's a uphill battle

and practical advice that readers can apply to their own lives.

"Life's Uphill Battle" also celebrates the small victories and moments of joy that make the journey worthwhile. I want to remind you that even in the midst of struggles, there are opportunities for growth, self-discovery, and finding meaning. They share stories of perseverance, hope, and the power of determination, showing readers that they are not alone in their struggles.

Ultimately, "Life's Uphill Battle" is a powerful reminder that life's challenges do not define us. It is a testament to the indomitable human spirit and the capacity to rise above adversity. With its uplifting message and practical insights, this book serves as a guidebook for anyone facing their own uphill battle, inspiring them to keep pushing forward, embrace the journey, and discover the strength within themselves.

Embrace challenges to maintain a positive attitude with determination

The journey is not easy, but it's a uphill battle

FINAL LETTER TO THE READERS:

"Don't Let Circumstances Define Your Journey"

I hope this letter finds you well. I am excited to introduce my self-help book, "Don't Let Your Circumstances Become Your Problem to Quit or Move Forward," and I am seeking representation to help bring this empowering message to a wider audience.

In a world where adversity and challenges are inevitable, it is easy for individuals to become overwhelmed and discouraged. However, my book aims to inspire readers to rise above their circumstances and take control of their own destinies.

Through personal anecdotes, practical strategies, and motivational insights, "Don't Let Your Circumstances Become Your Problem to Quit or Move Forward" provides readers with the tools and mindset needed to overcome obstacles and persevere in the face of adversity. It encourages readers to embrace a proactive approach to life, viewing challenges as opportunities for growth and transformation.

This book is not just another self-help guide; it is a roadmap for personal development and empowerment. It offers actionable steps for readers to cultivate resilience, develop a positive mindset, and harness their inner strength. By sharing stories of individuals who have

Embrace challenges to maintain a positive attitude with determination

The journey is not easy, but it's a uphill battle

triumphed over difficult circumstances, I aim to inspire readers to believe in their own potential and capabilities.

I believe that "Don't Let Your Circumstances Become Your Problem to Quit or Move Forward" has the potential to resonate with a wide audience. Its universal message of empowerment and resilience will appeal to individuals seeking motivation and guidance in their personal and professional lives.

Enclosed, please find the first three chapters of the book for your review. I am confident that once you delve into the pages, you will see the value and impact this book can have on readers. I would be thrilled to provide the complete manuscript for your consideration.

Thank you for considering my submission. I appreciate your time and consideration, and I look forward to the possibility of working together to empower individuals to overcome their circumstances and live their best lives.

Warm regards,

Embrace challenges to maintain a positive attitude with determination

The journey is not easy, but it's a uphill battle

"Mastering Your Mind: Conquering Daily Uphill Battles"

In our daily lives, we often encounter challenges and obstacles that can feel like uphill battles. Whether it's overcoming self-doubt, managing stress, or staying motivated in the face of adversity, mastering your mind is essential to navigating these challenges with resilience and determination.

In this empowering guide, we delve into the strategies and mindset shifts needed to conquer the daily uphill battles you face. By mastering your mind, you can transform challenges into opportunities for growth, self-discovery, and personal development.

Drawing on the principles of mindfulness, positive psychology, and self-improvement, this book offers practical tips and exercises to help you cultivate a resilient mindset and overcome mental barriers. From reframing negative thoughts to practicing self-care and building emotional resilience, you will learn how to harness the power of your mind to thrive in the face of adversity.

Each chapter explores a different aspect of mastering your mind, providing actionable steps and insights to help you navigate the ups and downs of daily life. Through real-life examples, inspirational stories, and expert

Embrace challenges to maintain a positive attitude with determination

advice, you will discover the tools and techniques needed to conquer your inner battles and emerge stronger on the other side.

"Mastering Your Mind: Conquering Daily Uphill Battles" is a transformative journey that empowers you to take control of your thoughts, emotions, and actions. By mastering your mind, you can unlock your full potential, cultivate a positive mindset, and approach each day with clarity, purpose, and resilience.

Are you ready to embark on this journey of self-discovery and empowerment? Read this book as we explore the power of mastering your mind and conquering the uphill battles that stand in your way. Together, we can embrace the challenges, overcome the obstacles, and emerge victorious in our pursuit of personal growth and fulfillment.

"Dependence on Self: Navigating Loneliness and Depression"

In the depths of loneliness and depression, when it feels like the world is against you, there is one constant source of strength that you can always rely on yourself. In this introspective journey of self-discovery and resilience, we explore the power of self-dependence in overcoming feelings of isolation and despair.

"Dependence on Self: Navigating Loneliness and Depression" is a heartfelt exploration of the inner strength and courage that lies within each of us, even in our darkest moments. Through personal anecdotes, practical strategies, and compassionate insights, this book serves as a guiding light for those who are struggling with feelings of loneliness and depression.

As you navigate the complexities of your emotions and wrestle with the weight of solitude, remember that you are not alone. By turning inward and cultivating a deep sense of self-dependence, you can find solace, comfort, and empowerment in your own company. This journey of self-reliance is not easy, but it is a powerful and transformative experience that can lead you towards healing and growth.

Through mindfulness practices, self-care techniques, and self-compassion exercises, you can begin to nurture a strong and resilient relationship with yourself. By acknowledging your worth, embracing your vulnerabilities, and honoring your emotions, you can gradually lift yourself out of the depths of loneliness and depression.

"Dependence on Self" is not about denying the support and connection of others but rather about recognizing the inherent strength and wisdom that resides within you. It is a reminder that even in moments of darkness, you have the power to light up your own path and guide yourself toward a brighter tomorrow.

As you embark on this journey of self-discovery and self-reliance, know that you have the resilience, courage, and inner resources to overcome loneliness and depression. By depending on yourself and trusting in your own ability to heal and thrive, you can emerge stronger, wiser, and more resilient than ever before.

The journey is not easy, but it's a uphill battle

"Rising Above Gossip: Defying Labels and Embracing Your Potential"

In a world where rumors and negativity can easily overshadow our true selves, it's essential to remember that external opinions do not define our worth or potential. "Rising Above Gossip" is a powerful reminder to stay true to yourself, defy labels, and embrace the limitless possibilities that lie within you, regardless of what others may say.

When faced with hurtful words and gossip, it's natural to feel discouraged and disheartened. However, it's crucial to recognize that the opinions of others do not hold power over your true identity or capabilities. By staying grounded in your values, beliefs, and strengths, you can rise above the noise and negativity that surrounds you.

In "Rising Above Gossip," we explore the transformative journey of self-discovery and self-empowerment in the face of criticism and judgment. Through personal anecdotes, empowering affirmations, and practical strategies, this book serves as a beacon of light for those who are navigating the murky waters of gossip and backbiting.

Embrace challenges to maintain a positive attitude with determination

As you navigate the complexities of interpersonal relationships and confront the shadows of gossip, remember that your worth is not determined by the words of others. By holding steadfast to your authenticity, integrity, and inner strength, you can transcend the limitations of gossip and reclaim your narrative with confidence and grace.

"Rising Above Gossip" is a testament to the resilience, courage, and unwavering spirit that resides within you. It is a reminder that you have the power to shape your own story, define your own worth, and unlock your full potential, regardless of the negativity that may try to hold you back.

As you embark on this journey of self-empowerment and self-acceptance, know that you are capable of rising above gossip, defying labels, and embracing the boundless possibilities that await you. Stay true to yourself, believe in your worth, and let your potential shine brightly, undeterred by the shadows of gossip that may try to dim your light.